The Economics of Sports

William S. Kern
Editor

2000

W.E. Upjohn Institute for Employment Research
Kalamazoo, Michigan 49007

Library of Congress Cataloging-in-Publication Data

The economics of sports / William S. Kern, editor.
   p. cm.
   Includes bibliographical references and index.
   ISBN 0–88099–210–7 (cloth : alk. paper) — ISBN 0–88099–209–3
   (paper : alk. paper)
    1. Professional sports—Economic aspects—United States. I. Kern, William S.,
   1952– II. W.E. Upjohn Institute for Employment Research.

GV583 .E36 2000
338.4'3796044'0973—dc21

00-040871

The facts presented in this study and the observations and viewpoints expressed are the sole responsibility of the authors. They do not necessarily represent positions of the W.E. Upjohn Institute for Employment Research.

Cover design by J.R. Underhill.
Index prepared by Nancy Humphreys.
Printed in the United States of America.

CONTENTS

Acknowledgments

The papers in this series were presented during the 35th Annual Lecture–Seminar Series presented by the Department of Economics of Western Michigan University during the 1998–1999 school year. The series is made possible through the generous financial support of the W.E. Upjohn Institute for Employment Research and the College of Arts and Sciences of Western Michigan University. I wish to express my gratitude to my colleagues on the Lecture Series Committee of the Department of Economics, Donald Alexander, and Wei-Chiao Huang for their support and encouragement.

Introduction

William S. Kern
Western Michigan University

Open to the sports pages of your local newspaper today and you are likely to find that discussions of the economic aspects of sports occupy as much space as do the results of the games. As Americans' discretionary incomes have risen, so has their demand for sports, as both participants and spectators. As a consequence of this increase in demand, we are now witness to professional athletes commanding long-term contracts of over $100 million. Cities are bidding against one another to acquire professional sports franchises with offers of new stadiums costing upwards of $500 million. Spectators are willing to pay "street prices" as high as $3,200 for tickets to the Super Bowl and $4,000 for tickets to college basketball's "Final Four." And professional sports owners and players' unions perennially talk about the possibility of strikes to resolve their differences over dividing up the multibillion dollar sports revenue pie. Clearly, sports has become "big business."

As the sports industry has grown, it has attracted the attention of economists, and sports economics is now a growing subfield within the economics profession. The organization of the sports leagues has been fertile ground for economists interested in industrial organization questions. The labor markets for professional athletes have been of interest to labor economists, given the abundance of statistics related to player performance and productivity and the unique features of these labor markets such as the National Basketball Association's (NBA) salary cap. The development of free agency in sports, the behavior of the National Collegiate Athletic Association in regulating collegiate sports, and the growing use of "personal seat licenses" by National Football League (NFL) teams have provided additional opportunities to observe and measure the effects of monopsony power, the behavior of cartels, and the practice of price discrimination.

1

Sports economics is also finding its way into the college class-room. Economists have found that sports is a useful medium for teaching economics, given the natural interest of many students in sports issues. The use of economic principles to help students understand the economic issues in sports provides evidence to students that learning economics can be both useful and fun. Thus, a small but growing number of colleges and universities now offer courses on the economics of sports.

The papers presented in this volume examine a number of contemporary economic issues in the world of sports. The lecture series that produced these papers was held at Western Michigan University during the 1998–1999 school year. The theme of the lecture series and this volume—"Economics of Sports: Winners and Losers"—is, of course, a play on words because it describes not only the results for the players of the game, but also the issues that we hoped the papers would explore. Though economists stress the desirability of outcomes that will improve the position of everyone, we are also aware that is not always the case. Indeed, many sports fans feel that they increasingly have come out losers as ticket prices have risen and they feel alienated from players who seem more interested in the money than the game. Cities that are vying to attract or retain sports franchises believe they will be winners in the game of urban development and job creation, but is that really the case? In the aftermath of the recent labor management struggles that have taken place in baseball and basketball, one wonders whether either side won!

The volume begins with a paper by Rodney Fort on the consequences of monopoly in professional sports. He argues that much of what sports fans complain about in pro sports—high ticket prices, high player salaries, and public subsidies for stadium construction—are predictable consequences of the monopoly power wielded by professional sports leagues. The monopoly power of sports leagues, he says, stems from the special legal treatment which sports leagues have been granted. The consequence of their special legal status is that leagues can restrict the supply of sports franchises, manage themselves as cartels, and stifle competition from competing sports leagues. The answer to this problem, Fort argues, is to apply a dose of competition to professional sports. He endorses a remedy for sports monopolies first offered by Ira Horowitz and Roger Noll—breaking up pro sports leagues into competing leagues.

One of the most hotly debated contemporary sports issues is the use of tax dollars by cities attempting to attract and retain professional sports franchises. Fort's paper reveals that this practice is a consequence of the monopoly power wielded by sports leagues, whose supply of franchises is limited relative to cities' demands. Thus, cities find that a new stadium, paid for with tax dollars, is the price to retain or attract a pro sports team. The stadium building boom also results from the belief that sports franchises are "hotbeds" of urban development that will generate jobs and growth. But is that really the case?

Professor Robert Baade is a pioneer in determining the impact of sports teams and stadiums on regional economies. In previous studies, Baade and others have found that the impact on regional growth and employment was negligible at best. In the paper presented here, Baade investigates the impact of sports facilities on neighborhood economies as well as their urban renewal strategy. Cities are building stadiums in the core city in an attempt to bring economic activity back to areas abandoned during the last several decades as population and economic activity have migrated to the suburbs. This has been a strategy followed by Cleveland, Atlanta, and Nashville where recently constructed stadiums were placed near the central business district, and in Detroit, where a new stadium for the Detroit Tigers was recently completed.

As a case study, Baade uses Seattle, which is constructing two new stadiums for the Mariners and Seahawks in close proximity to its former stadium, the Kingdome. Baade estimates the economic impact that the Kingdome's presence has had on the surrounding neighborhood, known as Pioneer Square.

If sports teams and new facilities generate negligible net increases in regional economic activity, and if, as Baade contends, they also do little to invigorate central business districts, then who are the primary beneficiaries of the public subsidies to sports franchises? This issue is addressed in the paper by John Siegfried and Timothy Peterson. They point out that in discussing stadium construction and team relocation, the public has focused on financing issues while economists have largely focused on efficiency issues. However, the equity issue remains largely unexamined. Siegfried and Peterson note that although some have complained that publicly financed stadiums amount "to constructing playgrounds for the rich," there is little objective evidence about the income distribution effects of these projects. They propose to remedy this by considering who bears the burden of the costs of new stadium construction and who receives the benefits.

The underlying theme of both Richard Sheehan's and Andrew Zimbalist's papers is the difficulty of maintaining competitive balance in sports. Although fans' enthusiasm is a function of the competitiveness of the leagues, gross mismatches in talent create dull contests which are not in the long-run interest of the leagues. However, success on the playing field is largely a result of a team's ability to acquire the most talented players and management's ability to provide the best facilities. Success is a function of the economic resources available to the individual teams, and these resources are often grossly unequal. Zimbalist points out that some teams in professional sports are located in cities that are eight times larger than other cities in the league. Major League Baseball is an obvious example of this problem. Small-market cities are finding it almost impossible to compete for talent with teams located in large markets.

Richard Sheehan's paper demonstrates that competitive balance is an issue in collegiate sports. He shows that, in contrast to the popular view of major collegiate sports, most college sports programs are not profitable. He considers the connection between the abilities of sports teams to generate revenues and their on-field success: in other words, is it possible to buy victories? And, will winning more make a school's sports programs more profitable? Sheehan argues that athletic finances and athletic success are intimately related. The ability to generate large revenues raises the likelihood of winning. However, increased winning often translates into small revenue gains. Sheehan thus argues that the "have nots" of college athletics are not likely to join the "haves" by investing in their college sports programs. A relatively small number of sports programs generate large sums of money and those programs perennially enjoy the bulk of on-field success.

Andrew Zimbalist's paper discusses the economic issues involved in the 1998–1999 NBA lockout. Zimbalist, who was a consultant to the NBA Player's Association during the negotiations, argues that there are several strategies that leagues might employ to preserve competitive balance. These include revenue sharing, skewing the reverse order of drafting of players to give poorer teams greater access to talent, artificially restricting the growth of players' salaries, and compelling league divestiture to engender competition.

The NBA owners claimed that the salary-cap restrictions they wished to impose were necessary to restore competitive balance by ensuring the survival of financially weak teams, but Zimbalist argues that this was mere rhetoric. Few, if any, teams were actually losing money, and those that were would soon have new arenas and more revenue from television. In addition, the owners attempted in both 1995 and 1998 to eliminate the Larry Bird exception, which was a device that helped to maintain competitive balance. The owners' argument, he concludes, was just cover for their attempt to raise profits by holding down the growth of salaries.

Zimbalist suggests that if the NBA owners are truly serious about the competitive balance problem, they should pursue the NFL's strategy of revenue sharing, but that faces serious obstacles in both basketball and baseball. The best solution, he argues, is one also suggested by Fort: foster competition by breaking up the existing leagues and creating new ones. With two leagues in each sport, large-market teams would have to share their market with teams from the competing leagues, and cities would not have to compete against one another by offering new stadiums to attract teams.

The volume concludes with a paper by Lawrence Kahn surveying the literature on the incidence of racial discrimination in pro sports with respect to salaries, hiring, retention, positional segregation, and customer prejudice. As Kahn points out, the world of sports has been a particularly rich environment in which to study discrimination because of the abundance of information related to player race, compensation, and productivity. Kahn's survey of the literature demonstrates that although the extent of discrimination appears to have declined over time, some evidence that discrimination in hiring, positional discrimination, and retention stemming from racial preferences of sports fans still lingers.

The six essays presented here offer a wide perspective on current issues in the field of sports economics from a group of scholars who have made significant contributions to this emerging field. They should certainly be worthwhile reading for anyone interested in the impact of sports teams and stadiums on urban development and in the attempts by professional and collegiate sports leagues to maintain competitive balance. We can only hope that some of the insights offered here will ultimately come to bear upon the decisions that the leagues and governments involved in these issues must make.

1

Market Power in Pro Sports
Problems and Solutions

Rodney Fort
Washington State University

Many Americans are completely carried away with sports. During the last baseball strike in 1994, Henry Aaron of the Brookings Institution (yes, there really is an economist with that famous baseball name) tried to put sports into perspective during his testimony before Congress. He pointed out that while the Major League Baseball (MLB) as an industry was just under $2 billion a year, the envelope industry topped the $2 billion mark. In a slightly broader view, the cardboard box industry generated well over triple that amount annually. He proceeded to lightly scold the subcommittee for spending its scarce and valuable time on such small potatoes.

Watching this testimony on C-SPAN, I was (very briefly) ashamed. After all, the importance with which I view sports is neatly summarized in one of my favorite Far Side cartoons. Artist Gary Larson shows a group of primordial sea-dwellers just off shore. One of the group holds a bat, and their baseball lies on the beach, just out of reach. The caption reads, "Great Moments in Evolution." The clear implication is that baseball is the reason we waddled out of the ooze in the first place. And here before Congress was an economist of no small renown pointing out that this inflated enthusiasm is over an industry that is dwarfed by only a small share of the paper products industry.

But my shame faded when I remembered that there is no cardboard box page in the daily paper. And it never has been the case that massive public subsidies for cardboard box companies have been on a referendum ballot. Sports really are different than cardboard boxes. Many of us enjoy benefits from sports that are vastly beyond what we spend on them. Whole other media industries thrive on its output, and it can be a consuming passion, this love of sports shared by so many. I think I might mail a copy of that Far Side cartoon to Professor Aaron.

This depth of feeling generates the concern of so many fans over the current state of pro sports. Talk to any sports fan and you will get at least one of the following opinions. Rising ticket prices threaten to slam the door on the average fan. Growing revenue imbalance leaves most teams out of contention before the season even starts. Stratospheric player salaries make it impossible to identify with players and introduces skepticism about whether or not they really lay it on the line every play. And do not even get a fan started about labor-management relations! MLB fans have recently lost their play-offs and a World Series because of them, and National Basketball Association (NBA) fans just lost half a season to labor unrest.

All of these outcomes are for the fans lucky enough to have a team. Many other fans have spent what seems an eternity waiting for an expansion team to arrive in their area. Others have seen their existing team threaten relocation at the drop of a hat. Team owners put all-or-nothing demands on their host cities and balk at every hint of intrusion into the power they wield over their sport. No other industry in the United States has such control over 1) exclusive geographical franchise rights over the entire industry, 2) team movement and location, 3) gate and TV revenue sharing, 4) TV contracts as a joint venture, and 5) entering talent through rookie drafts.

In the midst of all this unrest, you'll find economists nosing around. In our book, *Hardball* (1999), James Quirk and I organize the questions surrounding this fan frustration into a few chapters. Are the media and big TV money to blame? Is it player unions? Owners? Sports leagues? State and local politicians? Or what? As you can probably guess, we point our finger at "or what," which we define as market power.

Almost all economists see the ultimate culprit as market power, which derives from the special legal treatment of leagues. The outcomes are exclusive franchise rights for teams, management of sports leagues as cartels, and a complete stifling of any competing leagues, precisely those indicated by the basic economic theory of market power. In what follows, I will run through this logic and suggest what can be done about these outcomes.

Not much of what I am presenting here is new. Many of the issues were raised during the *Federal Baseball* decision of 1922, MLB's so-called antitrust exemption, enjoying its 75th anniversary this year.

Since that time, nearly all of these issues have been raised repeatedly in Congressional hearings that date back to 1951 and that represent at least 49 years of Congressional scrutiny. The ameliorative device proposed here also is not new. I found it first voiced in Congressional testimony by Ira Horowitz and Roger Noll in 1976. The problem is long-standing and one can only marvel that the current market power structure of sports leagues has withstood this scrutiny for so many years.

MARKET POWER PROBLEMS IN PRO SPORTS

Before proceeding to the heart of the matter—namely, market power—let us examine the more well-publicized culprits. Many claim that the media and big TV money cause most of the economic problems in sports. But the media are nothing more than a pipeline for advertising revenues, transporting them from advertisers, through broadcasters, and on to sports leagues and teams. There can be little doubt that the game on the field or floor is different because of television; there wouldn't be much point to on-field celebrations or taunting without an audience. But to networks, sports are just another type of programming that reaches particular demographic groups of interest to their advertisers. And, given that leagues can confront a small number of bidders with a chance at the rights to these important properties, it should come as no surprise that the bulk of the proceeds moves to the leagues and their teams. And this happens because leagues are allowed to act jointly in the sale of their TV rights, a practice that surely would be outlawed in any other industry.

Sportswriters are especially fond of making unions one of the major culprits in pro sports. Unions have no doubt changed the face of professional sports by removing nearly all of the mechanisms that owners previously used to restrict the free movement of players between teams. The result is that players now receive salaries much closer to the value of their contribution to team revenues. Some fans might begrudge players their huge salaries, but the money that fans spend on sports will not go away. If players don't get the money, then owners will keep it. In no small way, salaries are large because leagues earn more than the normal rate of return; it is the monopoly profit earned by leagues that is up for grabs in player–owner negotiations. Because players are free to move between teams without this profit, there wouldn't be much for a union to negotiate except minimum salaries and benefit packages. In summary, unions have not created the fabulous wealth available to athletes; they have just been proficient at moving that wealth from owners to players.

What about the players, themselves? Is their insatiable greed at least partly to blame for rising ticket prices? There is both a contradiction and a fundamental economic misunderstanding behind this view. First, for the interesting contradiction, why do fans think that players are any greedier than anybody else, including themselves? How many fans would be willing to take less than they could possibly make? Second, for the economic misunderstanding, sports salaries simply reflect the value that fans place on player talent. Player salaries are not the cause of high ticket prices or the rise of pay-per-view televised games. Instead, it is the willingness of fans to pay ever more for sports that raises player salaries and encourages owners to seek new avenues of collection like pay-per-view. Players are no more to blame for the high price of sports than movie stars are to blame for the rising price of movie tickets. According to economic theory, it is demand that drives the result. Besides, if players didn't take their share, would anybody reasonably suggest that owners would rebate the balance to fans?

So, it is not the media, or unions, or players who are responsible for market power problems. However, the source of the problem plaguing pro sports comes to light when we examine owners and their behavior together as a sports league. At the most basic economic level, owners possess the rights to a very valuable monopoly. That monopoly is granted by pro sports leagues, in plain view for all to see. Because leagues are allowed to behave like cartels in controlling inputs and outputs, individual teams in these leagues confront no current or future competition from rivals. The result for fans in this setting has been clear since the time of Adam Smith-restricted output, prices greater than marginal cost, and profits greater than the normal rate of return. Thus, it is not the personalities of owners that cause the economic problems in pro sports; it is in fact the leagues, which operate as one of the most successful monopolies in history.

That leaves politicians. Typically, when market power runs wild, we hope for political intervention to protect consumers, but, if anything, politicians have facilitated sports monopolies. First, despite the open invitation by Justice Holmes in his *Federal Baseball* decision, Congress has never intervened to define the antitrust status of MLB. Second, pro sports league mergers have been encouraged by Congress rather than denied. Finally, specific laws enacted by Congress, from local black-out laws to joint venture sale of TV rights, have served to cement the monopoly power of leagues. And it doesn't get any better at the local level. Witness the stadium mess plaguing so many current pro sports team hosts.

So, there you have it. Ticket prices are high because there are no competing teams in the same geographic market to push prices to marginal cost. Competitive balance is lacking because leagues restrict the number of teams in large revenue markets to the advantage of all league members. Salaries are higher than they would be under competition because some of the rents from market power accrue to players in a labor market that is carefully managed by unions. Strikes and lockouts occur as owners and players lock horns over the division of monopoly profits. Because leagues carefully manage the number of teams, output is restricted and prices rise, and some cities are purposely held open to solidify threats of relocation against current host cities. On the other hand, host cities are confronted with these all-or-nothing propositions because the careful management of alternatives by pro sports leagues has resulted in a lack of substitutes for professional sports teams. All this has occurred because market power has been allowed to dominate in pro sports.

Make no mistake about it. The value of market power in pro sports is high. When an owner buys a team, the price includes rights that are valuable beyond control of capital and a player roster. The new owner buys a monopoly right to provide the only game in a specific location as a member of the league. This right yields 1) gate, stadium, and local TV revenues; 2) any revenues that can be extracted from players; 3) special tax treatment; 4) a share of league-wide, national TV contract revenues; 5) a share of league earnings from expansion fees; and 6) spill-over benefits to other business enterprises of the team owner. In Los Angeles, the value of these rights recently was revealed at around $300 million during the sale of the Dodgers in 1998. In Cleveland, it was $530 million for the Browns in 1998. Abroad, it was nearly a $1 billion offer for the Manchester United soccer team in 1999.

There isn't any mystery about the remedy: a stiff dose of competition. However, this kind of economic competition is repulsive to owners and league personnel. National Football League (NFL) Commissioner Paul Tagliabue has been quoted as follows (*Sports Illustrated*, September 16, 1996), "Free market economics is the process of driving enterprises out of business. Sports league economics is the process of keeping enterprises in business." Quite aside from inventing a brand new term, *sports league economics*, the self-serving nature of the statement is only barely veiled. Before proceeding to a prescription for what ails pro sports, let us examine just what we would expect from a good stiff dose of competition.

ECONOMICALLY COMPETITIVE SPORTS LEAGUES

As Walter Neale (1964) pointed out long ago, the economics of sports indeed is peculiar. Cooperation is essential for the survival of sports leagues. They must cooperate in order to determine a schedule and a common set of rules and their enforcement. Appeals are essential, so some sort of cooperative central decisions are necessary. And, finally, leagues may need to cooperate to determine championship formats. But no one expects this cooperation to result in a restriction of output and prices exceeding marginal cost. That sort of cooperation is no more justified in pro sports than it is in any other economic endeavor.

Economic competition would tip the economic scales away from owners and players and toward fans and taxpayers. First, think about TV. Competition among leagues would eliminate monopoly profits from national TV contracts. Because a monopoly league can maximize TV revenues by restricting the number of games shown, introducing competition would result in more televised games. This would reduce the value of game broadcasts to advertisers because competition acts to bid away the profits earned from market power. Similarly, local TV revenue would decrease. Local broadcasters would go with the cheapest team of equal quality in their area. And the same argument applies to gate receipts. If fans could find substitute teams of equal quality, they would go with the one that charged least.

The impact of competition on player salaries is more difficult to determine. Players would no longer contribute to an economic activity that earned more than a normal return; therefore, players would be worth less. A further decline in player salaries would be expected from competition. Charles Finley, former owner of the Oakland Athletics, knew this well. He responded to player demands for free agency in the mid 1970s with a hoot. He suggested that MLB embrace this idea whole-heartedly because competition would kill the rising union tide and, along with it, salary arbitration and other artificial mechanisms propping up salaries. If competition removed sports unions from the picture, wages would fall even further. But there would be an important, off-setting factor. If leagues became truly and legally competitive, other restrictions on player earnings would not be expected to survive. For example, a rookie draft would wither away with the introduction of competition; this sort of restriction would not stand up to raiding by rival leagues. Thus, players in a competitive situation would be worth less than they had been under monopoly; and if their ability to organize were dealt a death blow as well, then their salaries might decrease further. But, this decline would be partly offset when other restrictions on earnings withered away under competition.

And while we are on the topic, most labor-management strife would disappear with competition because the major source of strife, monopoly profits, would be gone. Unions might still try raising pay for some players, which, in a competitive environment, would only increase owner costs and reduce overall player employment, but this behavior would be up to the union members themselves. The union focus might shift to pensions and other fringe benefits. And the already contentious issue of income distribution between superstars and journeyman players would increase.

Perhaps the most dramatic impacts of competition would occur in expansion and relocation. Under competition, all financially viable locations would have a team from one league or another. This would probably increase the number of teams in megalopolis markets and fans in these locations would enjoy more professional sports; but there would be a downside for other fans. Because gate and TV revenues would be lower, current marginal locations might become unprofitable. As always, with changes in market structure, there would be distributional consequences. Here, the trade-off would appear to be between the fans of marginal teams in a few cities and fans in larger areas.

State and local taxpayers also would feel the impact of competition on expansion and relocation. Because all viable locations would have a team, team owners would not be able to make threats about leaving their current host cities. In fact, the tables would take a dramatic turn: teams actually would compete for financially viable locations. If one team pushed its host too far, another team would be waiting in the wings for a lower subsidy. Competition should reduce subsidies to teams and possibly even put a market rental rate on existing and future publicly owned stadiums.

So, in a competitive economic environment, there would be more teams in big cities and a team in all economically viable locations. Cities would provide much lower subsidies, if any, in the form of extravagant stadiums and sweetheart stadium deals. The stadium mess would be alleviated. There would be more games on television, lower revenue to teams from television contracts, and lower ticket prices. Player salaries could either fall or rise, depending on the relative impacts of a few obvious labor market factors. Team profits would fall and franchise values along with them. In effect, power would be shifted from players and owners to fans and taxpayers. Some fans would enjoy more sports, while others would lose their team if it was just hanging on in the first place.

But economic competition has its limits, which must be considered when prescribing a remedy to the problem of market power in pro sports. First, there have been competitive leagues in the past, but the tendency has always been back toward a single, monopoly league. Economic competition has not been self-sustaining in pro sports, historically. Owners in rival leagues would ultimately see the value in reforming another monopoly; therefore, something more than just setting the wheels of competition in motion would be required to create change.

Another nuance to pro sports leagues also dictates caution in the prescription for market power. Existing leagues have already established their reputations and created a strong sense of fan identification. These teams suffered low or negative profits during their early years of growth and have paid public relations expenditures since that time. The returns on such an investment are the monopoly profits earned by these sports teams under their current league structures, and these returns have been earned for quite some time. A rival league planning to compete with existing leagues would have to make the same kind of investment, in addition to competing for talent to demonstrate that they really were an enduring, big-league alternative. This effort would be required in order to encourage fans and the media to commit their loyalties to their new league. But, if competition were enforced from the very outset for the new rival, the league would not be able to recover these costs. So, competition would not sustain itself, and it must be sustained externally in a very careful manner in order to nurture a rival.

In addition to the economic circumstances described so far, politics also impede economic competition in pro sports. As even the most casual student of government and the sports business knows, choices by elected officials often facilitate, rather than ameliorate, market power. Congress has failed to respond to the MLB antitrust court decision of 1922. In 1962, it exempted league-wide TV contracts in all sports from antitrust laws. Congress exempted the American Football League (AFL)–NFL merger from antitrust laws in 1966 and brought pressure to bear on the NBA to merge with the American Basketball Association (ABA) in the mid 1970s. Congress also has allowed other leagues to exercise veto power over the location of their teams. Now, leagues put teams where they want them and carefully control the most lucrative markets. Thus, despite repeated investigation, Congressional action has consistently enhanced monopoly power in sports, and state and local government outcomes have given us the stadium mess confronting so many current and prospective host cities.

CREATING ECONOMICALLY COMPETITIVE SPORTS LEAGUES

In summary, competition stands a better than decent chance of eliminating the ills in pro sports. But competition will not be self-sustaining, and in sustaining competition, one must exercise caution. Generating fan loyalty and staying power would be an expensive proposition for any new, competing league. Some long-term return would be required to make such an investment pay. An assurance of return would mean that special antitrust accommodations would be required because overzealous enforcement of competition would kill that return and the hope for competitive leagues. Finally, there is no reason to expect that federal, state, or local politicians would embrace a more economically competitive setting for pro sports. Politicians pursue reelection. Currently, that pursuit appears to favor the current market power status of leagues and we should not expect any change until politically potent opposition appears. A few voices crying in the wilderness is not enough.

For all but its political limitations, one plan would work. Suppose an existing league were simply broken up into competing leagues. The foundation is there already. The American and National leagues in baseball would be economically competitive if they were not under unified, cartel management by MLB. Indeed, prior to 1901, the two were, by and large, economic competitors! Essentially the same thing is true of the NFL. The American Football Conference (AFC) and the National Football Conference (NFC), with only a few cross-over teams, are precisely the most recent version of the AFL and the earlier NFL prior to the merger in 1969. The same would be true of the NBA and the National Hockey League (NHL). A breakup could restore much of the same competition that existed prior to their mergers with the ABA and the World Hockey Association (WHA), respectively. Therefore, a breakup of existing leagues could potentially create competing leagues.

But, again, one would not expect this situation to last on its own. Enforcement of these breakups under existing antitrust laws would be required for competition to flourish. If leagues tried to regroup and merge, antitrust enforcement should preclude their forming new cartels. Perhaps the most important element of a breakup/antitrust enforcement approach is that it would allow the resulting, competing leagues to retain the fan loyalty and media ties that they had cultivated over the years. The new leagues already are "major" in every sense of the word. And they wouldn't lose the fan identification that they have cultivated over the years. Interestingly though, one would expect that expenditures aimed at maintaining this loyalty would fall over time. The reason? The return on such investments would be falling under a competitive structure.

Of course, any movement away from monopoly would affect the welfare of leagues, players, fans, and taxpayers. Owners and players could be characterized as losers because their welfare will fall. Overall, fans would be winners because they would enjoy sports at lower prices, and taxpayers would win because subsidies would be reduced. However, some fans at locations with marginal teams might lose because competition would drive marginal teams out of business or to other locations.

One of the usual questions posed at this point is "What would be the quality of competition on the field with increased economic competition?" A long-standing "invariance principle," attributable to Simon Rottenberg (1956), suggests that quality will stay at its current level. After all, all of the earnings over and above the competitive rate were pure economic rents. Because the changes projected here would occur league-wide, players and coaches would face diminished opportunities wherever they turned in their sport. And their nonsport alternative would not have gotten any better. Would players play for less and coaches coach for less, rather than leave their sport? Almost certainly. Although the level of competition, while probably still unbalanced across a given league, would not be expected to decline.

Perhaps the minor leagues (baseball, basketball, and hockey) and college football, which operate at the same time and often in the same vicinity as major league teams, might prove instructive on the quality issue. Because economic competition would yield a different number and mix of teams of major league caliber, with more of them located in the largest cities, perhaps there would be a more continuous quality gradient between the current minor leagues and college conferences and the major leagues. Among the minor leagues and college teams, size and drawing power are similar to the determinants that would drive a competitive pro league structure.

But the nagging question is just how in the world will this ever happen. This idea of breaking up the major leagues dates back to Congressional testimony in 1976 by Ira Horowitz and Roger Noll, and still there has been no political action. This inaction is cause for pessimism among those interested in fixing the problems of market power confronting sports fans. However, market power and its consequences in pro sports must be good for politicians because it has been the norm for almost 100 years.

The environmental movement offers instructive lessons in changing the political status quo. When a problem becomes important enough to voters, they become politically mobilized. It is an expensive and laborious process. Those bent on such change must successfully accomplish an overwhelming educational mission. They must also overcome the high costs and free-riding behavior associated with organizing a politically potent group. After all of that, they face the dog-eat-dog world of advocate politics. Small wonder that market power has ruled in pro sports given the obstacles to bringing it down.

But maybe the times are changing. On the Internet, many fan advocate and alternative ownership arrangement pages have begun to appear; and the Internet dramatically reduces the costs of forming organizations. Further, while Major League Baseball appears to be rebounding from the strike of 1994, it could well be an illusory return driven mostly by the "Mark and Sammy Home Run Show." Dramatic revenue dispersion remains a source of tension between owners, and any additional interruption of play could bring down the wrath of fans. This wrath, however, might be a prerequisite to forming a politically potent interest group aimed at eliminating the market power in pro sports. Perhaps this organization might begin with the NBA, which is in turmoil. Their fans just lost half a season and are getting a weak imitation of the usual level of NBA play. If NBA fan interest groups rise to change the current local reelection margin, they may remedy the problem. For that is surely the only real solution. I hope I have made it clear that the culprit is market power. The rest is up to the fans, who, after all, are the source of nearly all of the profit in the first place.

References

Horowitz, Ira, and Roger Noll. 1976. *Inquiry Into Professional Sports*. Hearings before the House Select Committee on Professional Sports, 94th Congress, 2nd session, part 2. September 8, 9, 14–16, 21, and 22, pp. 133–136.

Neale, Walter. 1964. "The Peculiar Economics of Professional Sports." *Quarterly Journal of Economics* 78(February): 1–14.

Quirk, James, and Rodney Fort. 1999. *Hardball: The Abuse of Power in Pro Team Sports*. Princeton, New Jersey: Princeton University Press.

Rottenberg, Simon. 1956. "The Baseball Players' Labor Market." *Journal of Political Economy* 64(June): 242–258.

2

The Impact of Sports Teams and Facilities on Neighborhood Economies: What is the Score?

Robert A. Baade
Lake Forest College

INTRODUCTION

Among the noteworthy twentieth century trends identified for the United States has been the movement of people and economic activity from urban centers to the suburbs. Business has followed the migration of its labor force, and as a consequence most American city centers have deteriorated economically and socially in the latter years of this century. This urban economic malaise was further exacerbated in the 1980s by President Ronald Reagan's vision of a nation less dependent on a federal government. One manifestation of Reagan's emphasis on greater state autonomy was reduced federal revenue sharing. A less generous federal government translated into more parsimonious state governments, and, following the dollar food chain, less financial support for local governments. The erosion of the urban economic base compelled new economic strategies for cities, and mayors have responded by devising policies that emphasize the urban core as a cultural destination. Mayors hope that their cultural entrepreneurship will reverse the decades-old flow of people and money from city centers and serve to reestablish them as the hubs of American life. One aspect of this strategy has been the aggressive attempt by the mayors of many large cities to relocate professional sports stadiums from the suburbs to the central business districts (CBDs). The purpose of this study is to use the city of Seattle as a case study through which to analyze the prospects for improving economic performance in city centers by relocating stadiums used for professional sports to the CBD.

In addressing this issue, it is important to establish first the incidence of stadium migration from the suburbs back to the city center and to discuss the reasons for this development. In the next section of this study, the hypothesized microeconomic impact is contrasted with the macroeconomic or metropolitan impact. Scholars have studied the macroeconomic impact sufficiently so that reliable evidence is available on the influence professional sports have exerted on metropolitan areas. There are reasons, however, to expect that in terms of both magnitude and pattern, economic development at the local level may differ from that characterizing the metropolis. The next portion of the paper is devoted to discussing Seattle's use as a representative sample for exploring the likely economic impact of CBD relocation. Essential to this task is a brief discussion of Seattle's recent stadium history from the construction of the Kingdome to the present. The economic effect the Kingdome has had on the Pioneer Square Neighborhood, that portion of Seattle that borders the Kingdome on the West and North, is portrayed in the paper's next section. Critical to this analysis is a business survey largely conducted at the end of June 1998. Conclusions and policy implications are offered in the paper's final part.

STADIUM MIGRATION—BACK TO THE FUTURE

Earlier in the 20th century, stadiums were woven into dense urban fabrics. Rather than the stadium defining and shaping an area, the stadium was viewed as subordinate to a larger urban design and function. The existing city grid established the shape and location of many urban ballparks lending an idiosyncratic character to many of them. For example the Baker Bowl, home to the Major League Baseball's Philadelphia Phillies until 1938, was also known as "Hump" because it was built on an elevated piece of ground to accommodate a railroad tunnel running under centerfield (Lowry 1992). Today only Fenway Park in Boston (1912) with its legendary "Green Monster" and Wrigley Field in Chicago (1914) stand as representative monuments to past urban imperatives. Tiger Stadium in Detroit (1912) was recently replaced by a new ballpark, and discussions are under way to replace both Fenway Park and Wrigley Field.

In the post–World War II era, a rapidly expanding economy increased the personal incomes of most Americans to a point where former luxuries such as automobiles and houses outside crowded cities could be purchased by a majority of the population. As areas on the city's periphery were settled, businesses followed in part to capitalize on emerging markets for consumer goods and to gain proximity to the labor force. In keeping with this suburban trend, stadiums followed the fans. Expressways were built to accommodate the automobile, and suburban stadiums were located in close proximity to expressways to facilitate fan travel to the ballpark. Automobiles required space, and the typical suburban ballpark was surrounded by a sea of asphalt. The homes of most fans in the post–World War II era were connected to the ballpark by a seamless stream of concrete.

Accommodating the automobile came at a price from the perspective of the neighborhood in which the stadium was located. Easing entry and egress to the stadium mitigated the spillover of pedestrian traffic and economic activity into the environs where the ballpark was located. On the way from the stadium to their automobiles, fans encountered car windows not store windows. Once in their cars, the strong current of the expressways did not allow easy contact with commercial entities along the way. Any commerce that did occur in conjunction with sports spectating likely did so within the confines of the ballpark unless excursions into the neighborhood or elsewhere were planned.

Professional sports has been undergoing an economic revolution inspired by a confluence of circumstances both inside and outside the professional sports industry. These changes have affected both the supply and demand for professional sports, which, in turn, have had implications for where and how professional sporting events are packaged and presented. Nowhere are these changes more apparent than in the design and location of stadiums and arenas. Financial imperatives have worked to all but eliminate the multipurpose, circular stadium (the "ashtrays") built a few decades ago in cities such as Cincinnati, Pittsburgh, and Philadelphia to host both football and baseball. In addition, financial forces have reversed the trend toward locating ballparks in suburban areas with vast tracts of land suitable for inexpensive parking. Stadiums and arenas are coming back to the cities with promises of fan spending spilling over into the commercial corridors of the neighborhoods through which fans flow to reach transportation centers or remote parking lots.

Cities have used this promise of increased economic activity to persuade citizens to lend financial support to an aggressive city strategy to remake their centers into cultural destinations. For example, to lure people back to the downtown, Cleveland has developed the Gateway complex, which serves as a home to the Major League Baseball (MLB) Indians (Jacobs Field) and the National Basketball Association (NBA) Cavaliers (Gund Arena) along with the Rock and Roll Hall of Fame. Atlanta, Baltimore, Indianapolis, Minneapolis, and Nashville, to name but a few, are other cities that have opted for placing stadiums in or near the central business district (CBD) in an effort to help revitalize them. Stadium construction in the National Football League (NFL) symbolizes the return to downtown or near downtown locations. Barring unforeseen construction delays, 13 new stadiums will have been built in the 1990s. Of those, only facilities in Jacksonville (the renovation was of a scope sufficient to warrant it new), San Francisco, Tampa Bay, and Maryland (Washington Redskins) are located outside of what could be considered the CBD or CBD fringe. Approximately 60 percent of the NFL stadiums were located in or near CBDs prior to the 1990s, or about 16 percent less than characterize current construction trends. If the events conducted at the stadiums attract people from beyond the metropolitan areas in which they are located, then those who support public subsidies for these facilities promise that metropolitan, state, and regional economies will benefit from such investments. Do metropolitan economies derive a boost from professional sports and their stadiums? If they do, then surely the neighborhood in which the stadium is located is the recipient of those benefits. In the next portion of the paper, an assessment of the benefits accruing to the metropolis from professional sports teams and stadiums is analyzed.

TEAMS, STADIUMS, AND METROPOLITAN ECONOMIC IMPACT

The experience of a cross-section of cities across the United States over the past few decades strongly disputes the claim that professional sports teams and stadiums provide an economic boost for metropolises. Baade (1996) found no correlation between the real growth differential in real per capita personal income for a city experiencing some change in its professional sports industry and cities experiencing no such change or having no professional sports presence. Baade's analysis included all cities hosting a team in one of the four major professional sports (baseball, basketball, football, and hockey), and covered more than three decades of observations beginning in 1958. All else equal, one would expect a professional sports host city to expand economically if sports does attract more than local interest and dollars. The fact that evidence fails to support such a contention requires an explanation and several come immediately to mind.

First, the professional sports team may simply be too small to influence in any meaningful way a large, diverse metropolitan economy. For example, in litigation regarding the constitutionality of using several hundred million dollars of public funds for subsidizing a new stadium for the NFL's Tampa Bay Buccaneers to replace a 20-year-old facility, the author testified as an expert representing those opposed to public subventions that the team's revenues ranked below more than 70 other enterprises in that city. In using an academic context to provide perspective, Noll and Zimbalist (1997, p. 57) observed that the top ten universities in the United States received $2.8 billion in federal grant money in 1994, which was more than the combined revenue of the NFL and National Hockey League (NHL) or the combined revenue of MLB and the NBA for that year.

Second, and perhaps more important, consonant with elementary budget constraints, spending on professional sports spectating substitutes for time and money that could be spent on other goods or services. To the extent that the fan base is largely indigenous to the metropolitan area, net spending in the metropolitan area may increase, decrease, or stay constant even though gross spending on sports increases significantly. The distinction between gross and net spending changes is pivotal in precisely estimating the impact of professional sports. Some economic impact studies supporting stadium subsidies use a gross measure of spending that occurs in conjunction with professional sports. They then purport to capture the indirect impact through "multiplier analysis."[1] A measure of net spending changes, of course, requires substantially more data or more sophisticated modeling and accounts in part for the use of estimates of gross spending to defend stadium subsidies. Given the paucity of data and the complex web of financial inflows and outflows that occur as a consequence of hosting a professional sports team, a reasonable estimate of the team's economic contribution likely can be rendered only through comparing the metropolitan economic landscape before and after the team or stadium. This after-the-fact audit in estimating the economic impact of professional sports has been favored by some economists (Noll and Zimbalist 1997; Baade and Sanderson 1997; Hamilton and Kahn 1997; Austrian and Rosentraub 1997).

Estimates on gross and net new spending differ substantially. For example, in a report estimating the economic impact of the Seattle Mariners on the city of Seattle, King County, and the state of Washington prepared by Dick Conway & Associates for King County in 1994, net direct spending as a percentage of gross direct spending was identified as 44.3 percent for the city and county ($40.4 million/$114.0 million for both the city and the state) and 32 percent ($29.1 million/$114.0) for the state (Conway and Byers 1994). The difference between gross and net total direct economic impact are more pronounced because multipliers will compound differences in gross and net measures of direct economic impacts. Total net economic impact as a percentage of total gross economic impact as calculated by Conway & Associates was 23.9 percent ($42.9 million/$179.7 million), 38.5 percent ($53.3 million/$138.8 million), and 40.1 percent ($47.7 million/$119.1 million) for the state, county, and city, respectively.

In relative terms, gross economic impact is likely to be most pronounced in the neighborhood in which the stadium is located. In measuring the impact professional sports has on economies, a circle could be drawn from the point where the event actually occurs, and it could be argued reasonably that the magnitude of the impact, in relative terms at least, varies inversely with the size of the circle. Stated somewhat differently, the economic effect is thought to be most pronounced at "ground-zero," the exact location of the event. As the circumference of the circle expands, the net impact diminishes as the dollars spent on the sporting event are more completely offset by reduced spending elsewhere. Following this budgetary logic as it relates to leisure spending, the global impact of even the largest sporting events such as the Summer Olympics approximates zero if an increase in global net spending is not induced by the event itself. This is true because even those who come from great distances spend time and money at the Olympics in lieu of time and money they would have spent elsewhere. The impact locally, therefore, depends on the extent to which spending and respending occurs by those residing outside the environs where the event is held, or by local citizens who spend money on the sports event as opposed to spending discretionary income outside their neighborhood. Theoretically, a local government might decide to subsidize sports if the audience is distinctly nonlocal. In the case of Seattle, Pioneer Square (the neighborhood in which the Kingdome is located) might be given an economic boost if those who view the professional sports events hosted by the stadium are either living outside the community or are residents who would spend discretionary dollars outside Pioneer Square. Within the neighborhood, there are outflows associated with team and stadium activities, and so even at the local level, professional sports might fail to provide much of an economic boost. Later in this chapter, I assess the economic impact the Kingdome has had on Pioneer Square. First, however, it is appropriate to identify why Seattle is worthy of study.

WHY SEATTLE?

Seattle typifies the contemporary economic relationship that U.S. cities hosting major league sports have with their teams, particularly as it relates to stadiums. In less than two decades after its construction, owners of the NFL Seahawks and the MLB Mariners declared the Kingdome economically obsolete. In their opinion, the Kingdome could not compete financially with the new breed of stadiums being built across the country. In citing a general shortcoming of multipurpose stadiums, the Kingdome's critics argued that it failed to provide an environment that encouraged fans to return because it compromised sight lines for individual sports and otherwise reduced the ambiance associated with single-sport structures, e.g., Wrigley Field in Chicago.

Most important, however, was the relative paucity of luxury seating and other revenue-generating amenities that the owners argued placed their teams at a distinct financial disadvantage. Failure to compete financially limited their ability to compete for free-agent talent and all but assured mediocrity on the playing field, which would further erode the team's financial standing. Echoing this well-rehearsed line, the owners contended that Seattle's parsimony gave them no choice but to consider the offers of other suitor cities throughout the United States. The price to Washingtonians to keep the teams would be steep: separate stadiums for the Seahawks and Mariners outfitted with state-of-the-art amenities, including a retractable dome for the Mariners' facility. Even though a majority of the citizens of Seattle voted "no" in a referendum to build a stadium for the Mariners, new stadiums are now under construction for the Mariners and Seahawks. The cost for both facilities will likely eclipse $700 million.

The apparatus of persuasion employed in trying to convince the people of Seattle that this was not an egregious example of corporate welfare included the claim that the stadiums should be considered investments. As such, boosters noted that the facilities did not force painful civic tradeoffs such as financial neglect of schools, streets, and sewers but would instead generate a stream of revenues that could be invested in many forms of public infrastructure. Owners, players, and fans would not be the only winners, apologists for the stadiums claimed, citizens of the metropolis and state would benefit as well. The economic impact studies commissioned by new stadium proponents typically identify thousands of new jobs, more than $100 million of economic impact, and substantial increases in tax revenues at all levels of government as the outcome of spending on a professional sports team (Conway and Byers 1994). In opposition to these data, and as noted in the previous section, other scholarly studies have debunked the myth of sports serving as significant catalysts for metropolitan economic development. However, the claim that substantial local or neighborhood economic development occurs endures. What has been the experience of the neighborhood in which the Kingdome is located? What are the magnitude and pattern of local economic development inspired by the Kingdome, and what will the new stadiums do for the environs in which they are located? The next portion of the paper addresses these questions.

THE KINGDOME AND LOCAL ECONOMIC IMPACT

The now-razed Kingdome and site for the two new stadiums is bordered on the north and west by Pioneer Square, a neighborhood of historical significance and of a mixed commercial and residential character. Pioneer Square covers a 90-acre area roughly demarcated by Cherry and Marion Streets on the north, 2nd and 3rd Streets on the East, the Alaskan Way and the waterfront on the west, and Royal Brougham Street on the south. Figures 1 and 2 show the location of Pioneer Square, including the Kingdome. Because the stadiums that will replace the Kingdome are under construction just south of it, this map can be used to provide a reference for placing the new stadiums in Seattle.

Pioneer Square exhibits significant diversity with respect to its inhabitants and business enterprises. Missions for the homeless and condominiums for city officials exist within blocks of one another. There are 849 housing units in Pioneer Square and roughly 1,200 full-time residents. This low ratio of residents to housing units is explained in part by the high number of units that are identified as single room occupancy (SROs). In addition to this low income housing, there are 737 shelter beds, but those who occupy them are not considered full-time residents. There are 600 businesses in the business improvement area (BIA) of Pioneer Square. Sports bars and jazz clubs share street space with art galleries and a store that has provided leather goods for more than a century for people who use horses for more than entertainment. Fifteen surface parking lots and six parking garages provide for the parking needs of residents, workers, and visitors to the neighborhood. The skeletal structures of the new stadiums are rising in what used to be the far southern parking lot serving the Kingdome. Prior to the construction of the new stadiums, the Kingdome parking lots provided space for approximately 3,600 cars.[2] The Kingdome seated 66,400 people for football, and even at the conservative ratio of one parking space for every four fans, when the stadium was filled to capacity, 16,600 parking spaces were required. This stadium parking shortfall had substantial implications for the neighborhood. Parking issues will be discussed extensively in the next section of the paper.

Figure 1 Pioneer Square Business Improvement Area

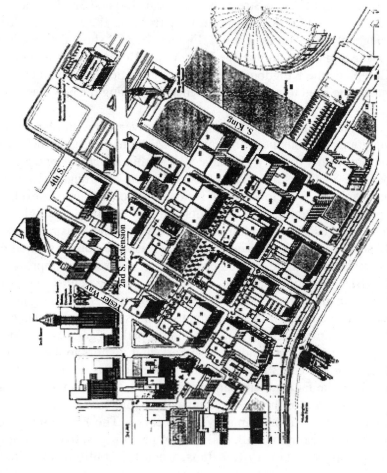

SOURCE: The Pioneer Square Business Improvement Area; used with permission.

Figure 2 Seattle Neighborhoods

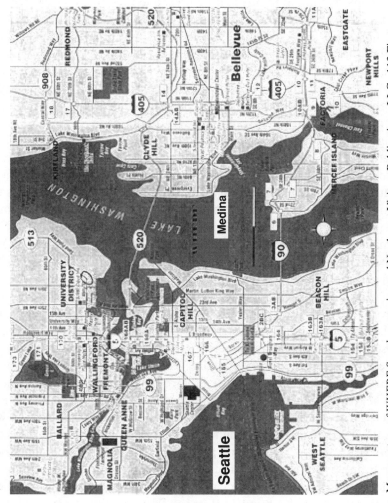

Map courtesy of *WHERE Seattle* magazine and Northwest Visitors Publications, LLC., 113 First Avenue N., #200, Seattle, WA 98109, est. 2000.

The decision to raze the Kingdome was based in large part on the need to provide parking for the patrons of the new stadiums.

The Kingdome originally cost $69 million. It underwent two renovations in the 1990s. One of the renovations centered on structural problems relating to falling ceiling tiles, and the other concentrated on shoring up a foundation that ostensibly made the facility vulnerable to earthquakes. The cost of these two corrective projects exceeded the $69 million spent to build the Kingdome. The price for the new stadiums has not been determined because cost overruns are already materializing. As mentioned previously, the price for both of them will very likely exceed $700 million. Boosters justify these substantial investments in stadium infrastructure to residents of the Pioneer Square neighborhood, the city of Seattle, King County, and the state of Washington. They note how the substantial amount of economic activity directly and indirectly related to the Kingdome will benefit all Washingtonians. As noted previously, ample empirical evidence negates the notion that these sizeable investments will positively affect the Seattle metropolitan and state of Washington economies. The question remains, however, did the Pioneer Square neighborhood benefit on balance from having the Kingdome in its backyard? And what does the answer imply about the impact of the new stadiums?

Based on the demographic characteristics, Pioneer Square has relatively few full-time residents with the financial wherewithal to buy tickets to professional sporting events. It follows that the sports events hosted by the Kingdome attracted the majority of their fans from outside Pioneer Square. If the spending that occurred in conjunction with sports remained in the Pioneer Square economy, the local financial boost provided by the stadium would have been substantial. The key, of course, is the extent to which the money spent by nonlocal fans was locally retained and spent again and again in the neighborhood. Those who assert that the Kingdome provided a substantial economic boost for Pioneer Square likely focused their attention on the financial inflows only. Casual empiricism supports the assertion that the Kingdome represented a boon to Pioneer Square. On event days, fans streamed into the stadium and the environs and spent large amounts of money. A precise rendering of the economic impact, however, requires not only an accurate measure of the dollars spent on sports spectating and related activities, but a thorough identification of the money outflows that occurred as a consequence of Kingdome events as well. The financial leakages from the neighborhood economy may well have been substantial, and can be broadly categorized as 1) earnings repatriated by owners, players, and other team and stadium personnel to their residences; 2) the costs incurred to operate the stadium to include the opportunity costs; and 3) business losses incurred locally as a consequence of peak usage of local resources on game day. Stated somewhat differently, local business activity may have been crowded out.

The Pioneer Square neighborhood, to be sure, experienced significantly more economic transactions as a consequence of the Kingdome. Assume for the moment that we think of Pioneer Square as a business entity and that we identify the Kingdome as a part of Pioneer Square's stock of capital.[3] From this business, capital stock income flowed when tickets, baseball paraphernalia, and hot dogs were sold. The economic impact, however, was not equal to gross spending changes any more than revenues are equal to business profits. Explicit and implicit costs arose as a consequence of conducting events at the Kingdome, and the economic contribution that the Kingdome made to Pioneer Square was not consonant with gross financial inflows but rather with net financial inflows to the neighborhood. Two facts may well serve to vitiate the economic impact the operation of the Kingdome would at first blush appear to provide. First, the stadium may have served as little more than an economic conduit through which spending on Kingdome events passed from one set of nonresident hands to another. Second, the level and urgency of game day activities may have well strained local resources by crowding out local, normal business activity. If either of these effects were pronounced, the neighborhood in which the stadium was located would have derived far less stimulation than that suggested by the direct spending that occurred within the stadium's walls.

The first point can be illustrated through tracing player salaries. A stadium does not resemble the corner grocery where the owners live above the store. Rather the stadium owners and the stadium employees, who receive most of the event revenues, are in all probability not neighborhood residents. Thus even if fans are not residents and their spending represents an infusion of funds, the boost provided is short lived because the nonresident owners and players appropriate that spending in the form of their profits and wages. Recent developments in professional sports as they relate to stadium construction may well be making the transfer of funds from one group of nonresidents to another more complete. In negotiations with their host cities, teams have more aggressively and thoroughly exploited the advantage imparted by an excess demand for teams. The new breed of stadiums have evolved into small walled cities that more completely compete with and capture the economic activity that used to spill out into the neighborhood. This stadium/mall concept has been encouraged by the leagues to help level the financial playing fields of league members. Furthermore, in their anxiety to attract or retain their teams, cities have been agreeing to more generous leases that allow teams to appropriate virtually all of the revenues from ticket sales, concessions, the sale of sports paraphernalia, parking, stadium advertising, and naming rights. The quid pro quo for these "sweetheart" leases is that the team dedicate one revenue source or another to satisfy public demands for a team "equity" stake in the ballpark project. Teams readily agree because the present value of increased stadium earnings exceeds by a significant amount the present value of the dedicated revenue stream(s).

Owners have argued that stadiums are necessary to satisfy player demands for higher salaries. Suppose for the moment that this owner rationale is true. Today for the NBA and NFL, the two sports leagues that first instituted salary caps, the share of league gross revenues to which players as a group are entitled by agreement is 57.5 and 63 percent of league gross revenues, respectively. It follows, therefore, that significantly more than half of the spending that occurs at the ballpark finds its way into the pockets of players. If players do not live in the community or otherwise do not spend on community goods and services, then more than one-half of the revenue that finds its way into the stadium on game day leaks from the neighborhood. In the case of Seattle, it is a virtual certainty that few, if any, of the Seattle Seahawks' owners and players live in Pioneer Square. In fact, the market for players is national, many of them do not establish their primary residences in the cities in which they play. Players invest their earnings internationally and are taxed nationally, therefore, much of what they earn leaves not only the Pioneer Square economy but the metropolitan economy as well.

The point made through tracing player salaries applies to taxes imposed by nonlocal government. Ignoring for the moment "home rule," how much of the sales tax on sports clothing or excise taxes on game tickets is retained by the local government? Much of it becomes a part of general revenues for the State, County, or City government imposing the tax, and the extent to which it is returned to the local government depends on institutional arrangement. The local governments which provide space for the stadium need to have a hand in shaping revenue sharing to ensure that their costs for providing stadium space are covered. They also must understand the extent to which the stadium and team activities affect general tax revenues at higher the levels of government from which they derive a share. Such an analysis is hardly trivial, but it must be undertaken if the neighborhood is to make wise decisions with regard to the use of its scarce land resource.

Opportunity and operating costs, as well as the likelihood that stadium activity will "crowd out" local economic activity, depend on the character of the neighborhood economy. Is there a natural synergy between the stadium and neighborhood, or will expenses mount and displacement and inactivity occur on a scale that ensures the cost of hosting the stadium exceeds the expected benefit? Stadiums require large tracts of land not only for structures but also for parking if the stadium site or the institutional character of the metropolis or region makes it accessible primarily by automobile. Stadiums are not like shopping malls where economic activity occurs throughout the course of a day every day. Stadiums, particularly open-air football stadiums, spend more time waiting than working. How the community handles the "dead time" in the stadium and its attendant areas is critical to its ability to use the facility to its economic advantage. Did the Pioneer Square neighborhood and the Kingdome enjoy a synergistic relationship? If not, could the lack of synergy have been anticipated by analyzing the community's economic character? To help establish the fit between the neighborhood and the stadium, a survey was conducted to assess the impact of the Kingdome on local businesses. The survey is appended to the paper, and the results of it are discussed in the next section of the paper.

SURVEY RESULTS AND IMPLICATIONS

Compared with other districts in Seattle, the Pioneer Square district is more commercially diverse. Although retail businesses are most prevalent within the Business Improvement Area (BIA) of the district, constituting 20.3 percent of all businesses, there are significantly fewer than in other districts such as Broadway and Roosevelt, which exhibit retail percentages of 56 and 54 percent, respectively. Professional services, legal services, and art galleries account for 17.6, 13.1, and 9.2 percent, respectively, of all businesses within the Pioneer Square BIA (krs services, inc. 1998). Figures 3 and 4 define the Pioneer Square urban village footprint and the Pioneer Square BIA boundaries, respectively (krs services, inc. 1998).

In comparing the character of the businesses in Pioneer Square with businesses in other districts in Seattle, several attributes distinguish the enterprises of Pioneer Square. The businesses in the Kingdome neighborhood tend to have had shorter histories, are more labor intensive, exhibit a greater tendency to rent their commercial spaces, and are smaller. To wit, 86 percent of the businesses within the BIA gross less than $1 million per year (krs services, inc. 1998). All of this indicates that the businesses of Pioneer Square are more fragile in general than enterprises in other districts in Seattle. Where controversial urban projects are concerned, this is not inconsonant with national trends. Districts that are successful in preventing the development (airports, incinerators, and stadiums) from occurring in their neighborhood ("not in my backyard") are generally populated by commercial interests that are big, established, wealthy, and politically connected. Downtown stadiums are generally constructed in warehouse or old railroad yards where land is relatively cheap and political resistance is relatively feeble. These fringe downtown areas, however, are often in the incipient stages of development or have clear alternative uses. The concern of residents and local entrepreneurs in such areas is that the stadium may channel development in directions that are not compatible with the emerging pattern of growth. The survey results indicated that the activities at the Kingdome frustrated rather than contributed to many business activities in Pioneer Square. The reason cited in every

Figure 3 Pioneer Square Urban Village Footprint Boundaries

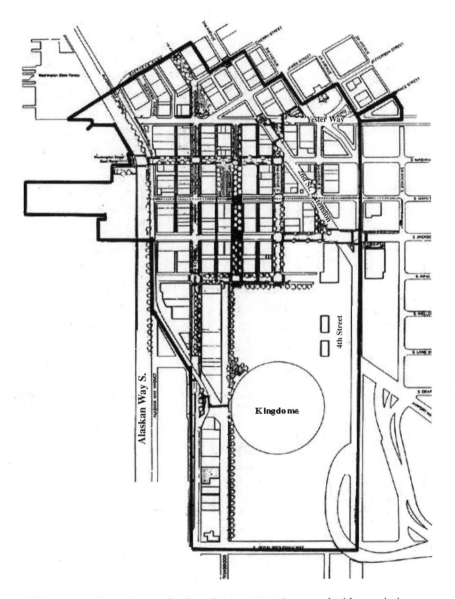

SOURCE: The Pioneer Square Business Improvement Area; used with permission.

Figure 4 Pioneer Square Business Improvement Area Boundaries

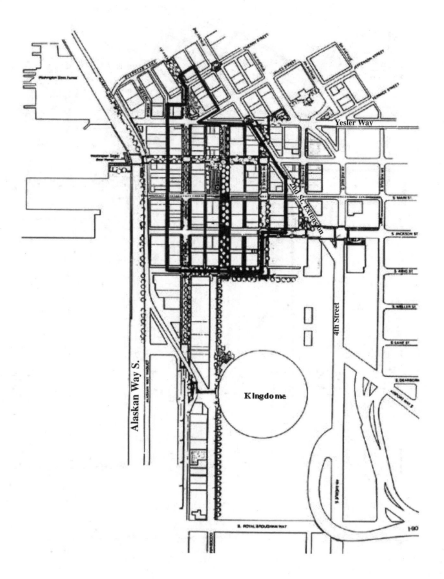

SOURCE: The Pioneer Square Business Improvement Area; used with permission.

instance of business disruption had to do with parking and general congestion created by events at the Kingdome.

Table 1 provides the result of the survey conducted in Pioneer Square June 26 through June 30, 1998.

Table 1 Reported Percentage Changes in Revenues for Businesses in Pioneer Square as a Consequence of the Kingdome[a] ($n = 35$)

Business type	Decrease by more than 25%[b]	Decrease by less than 25%	Remain constant	Increase by less than 25%	Increase by more than 25%
Eating and drinking places[c]		2	5	2	6
Hotels, motels			1[d]		1
Art galleries	2	2			
Clothing, jewelry and other retail[e]	3	1		1	1
Professional services to include legal	1		3		
Entertainment, discos, tourist attractions		2	2		
Total	6	7	11	3	8

SOURCE: Author's survey.

[a] If the results for the Mariners and Seahawks differed, the convention used was to report the baseball result for two reasons. First, many businesses were not open on Sundays when the Seahawks normally play. Second, the baseball Mariners had 81 home dates compared to eight regular season games for the Mariners. There were 10 cases in which businesses were open on Sunday and reported different impacts (degree, not direction) for the Mariners and Seahawks.

[b] Percentage changes are reported to insure autonomy for the businesses that participated in the survey.

[c] In general, the eating and drinking establishments closest to the Kingdome benefited most from its operation. The impact, in general, diminished with each additional block of distance.

[d] Hotel located outside the Pioneer Square footprint.

[e] Those retail outlets that reported an increase in sales were both in the business of selling sports paraphernalia.

Several conclusions can be drawn based on the survey and interviews of businesses in the Pioneer Square BIA. First, bars that have a sports theme and a location adjacent to the Kingdome derived substantial benefits. Sports bars/restaurants in the immediate vicinity of the Kingdome reported as much as an 800 percent increase in revenues from Mariners' games on weekdays and an increase in business by 1700 percent from weekend Mariners games. Second, the increase in the bar/restaurant business generally was inversely related to the establishment's distance from the Kingdome. Unless the bar had a particularly compelling sports identity, three or four blocks walking distance from the stadium was sufficient to eliminate most of the positive economic impact cited by bars a block or less away. Proximity, however, is no guarantee of success. If the bar/restaurant was not on a pedestrian thoroughfare, the impact was also muted. To cite an example, one bar/restaurant a block and one-half from the stadium, but removed from the constellation of bars frequented by fans after a game, attempted to build a clientele with sports promotions and themes with no success. The bar has changed hands four times in the past few years due to a lack of business. Third, the success of the sports bar/restaurant is highly sensitive to the success of the teams. Not only does a winning team attract more fans to the stadium, but apparently fans supporting mediocre or losing teams are in no mood to celebrate. Several sports bars that gushed about the positive impact of the Mariners and Seahawks sounded a much more sober note in describing the Mariners impact on business in 1998 and other years in which the teams did not compete for a championship.

Other businesses did not share the enthusiasm or the success of the sports bar entrepreneurs for the Kingdome and its teams. Ethnic restaurants, art galleries, professional services, legal services, and most retail outlets reported a decline in business generally in the neighborhood of 25 percent or less. Some professional service establishments, including law offices, have considered changing their location because of the difficulties they encounter meeting clients on game days. The culprit cited by all firms adversely affected by the Kingdome was inadequate parking.[4] As noted previously, the Kingdome parking lots were insufficient to meet the peak traffic flow during stadium events. Automobiles spilled into the neighborhood crowding out normal business activity by using scarce parking spaces. If local spending that occurs in conjunction with the stadium events equaled or exceeded local spending that would occur in the absence of the stadium events, then on balance the local economy would gain. The means for measuring the net spending change are inadequate, but it is clear that the stadium activity did channel business into certain realms and away from others and did create the need for additional parking.

The demand for parking for peak neighborhood activity connected with stadium events creates a dilemma for the community. On one hand, building more parking structures or surface lots minimized the economic disruption caused by the excess demand for parking. On the other hand, using scarce land to accommodate peak parking demand for a few hours of approximately one hundred days would change the character of the neighborhood. Also, providing for more parking would likely create negative externalities and "public goods" issues that would be esthetic as well as economic in nature. Parking lots are strictly utilitarian. They are not attractive structures and have no particular architectural character.

A second option is to price the parking to discourage the quantity of it demanded. One of the bitterest complaints relating to the Pioneer Square parking problems is the increase in parking prices on game day. Participants in the survey reported that lot parking rates double on game or event days and that "meter maids" get more aggressive, thus raising the implicit parking price. The parking problem could be exacerbated further because two stadiums will replace the Kingdome. No agreement has been reached to prohibit the use of the two stadiums on the same day. If events are held on the same day and are highly attended, then the parking problem could escalate dramatically. Despite what is now the north parking lot will be used for housing, government has promised that the number of parking spaces in the Pioneer Square area will be increased through the construction of at least one new tiered parking lot. Of course, tiered parking structures are far more expensive than surface lots, and egress from them is slower.

The parking problem can be mitigated if the public opts for using the area public transit. Union Station (rail) and the International District Station for the International Transit Tunnel (bus) are a few blocks northeast of the dome. The Pioneer Square Station of the Downtown Transit Tunnel is only a few blocks further away from the Kingdome. Closing some streets to parking on game day and raising parking prices is designed, in part, to encourage transportation to the stadium using some means other than automobiles. It should be noted that the use of public transportation requires a significant cultural modification. It is arguable that people in the western part of the United States are unusually partial to automobile transit and display a reluctance to use public transportation. How much inconvenience or additional expense will be required to motivate them to opt for alternative transportation? That question is being debated by people not only in Seattle but throughout the West and the entire United States. Because 50 percent of the businesses inside the BIA and 90 percent of the businesses ringing the BIA indicated that transportation was critical to their business (krs services, inc., 1998), the automobile transportation problem as it relates to Pioneer Square has to be resolved. Parking validation programs for residents and business customers, shuttle buses for neighborhood employees, and park and ride (satellite parking) programs are being seriously considered.

In summary, the results of our survey indicated that less than one-third of the businesses located in Pioneer Square reported revenue increases attributable to the Kingdome. Aside from the parking lot business, bars and restaurants with a sports identity benefited, as did Pioneer Square hotels. In general, however, most businesses located in Pioneer Square (retail, professional services, legal services, and art galleries) reported that their revenues either remained constant or suffered as a consequence of the Kingdome. This finding echoes results reported in the recent survey conducted by krs services, inc. On page 13 of their July 24, 1998 study, the firm reported:

> It is interesting to note that lack of dependence by the majority of Pioneer Square businesses on tourists, spectators at sporting/Kingdome events and participants in the First Thursday or gallery activities . . .
> It is also interesting that, according to those who participated in the survey, there appears to be as much business reliance on customers attending First Thursday or patronizing art galleries as there are spectators attending sporting events or other activities at the Kingdome.

Reportedly, the Kingdome adversely affects certain businesses in Pioneer Square because of its peak use of key community resources, most notably parking, during stadium events. In general, the stadium's overall economic impact on the neighborhood was uncertain. Therefore, with any new urban stadium, overall economic activity could increase, remain constant, or decrease. What is clear is that city governments cannot assume that the influx of spectators into a neighborhood for a stadium event will translate into increased economic activity to a degree commensurate with the number of visitors. Indeed, in identifying the reasons why a stadium may not induce an expansion of the metropolitan economy, one may not have to look any further than the neighborhood in which the stadium is located. In the neighborhood, the substitution effects, which negate the impact of fan spending in conjunction with the sporting events, are most apparent.

CONCLUSIONS AND POLICY IMPLICATIONS

There appears to be growing agreement that professional sports teams and stadiums have little if any economic impact on their host cities. The lack of economic impact is explained by simple budgetary realities. If the fans attending the sporting events are indigenous to the city hosting the event, then the time and money they spend spectating at sporting events is vitiated by reduced spending elsewhere within the metropolitan area. The impact on the local or neighborhood economy in which the stadium is located is less clear. The influx of nonresidents on game or event day suggests substantial economic impact. Does more careful empirical analysis confirm casual observation? Does the downtown benefit from the construction of a sports stadium?

The evidence from Seattle is decidedly mixed. Clearly the stadium channels economic activity in the direction of businesses that have a connection to sports. Stadium bars and restaurants and retail outlets selling sports paraphernalia benefit. Many other businesses, particularly those that do not appeal to sports fans, lose business. This occurs as a consequence of peak use of shared community resources on event day; parking and sidewalk space are the most obvious examples. Customers that ordinarily would patronize local businesses do not on event day because the cost and inconvenience of doing so increases. Routine or normal business, therefore, is crowded out on a scale that may well offset any neighborhood gains. Unless the excess demand for key local resources is somehow mitigated, many other commercial activities in the neighborhood are destined to decline.

The policy implications are clear. Whether the stadium contributes meaningfully to the local economy depends on the nature of that economy and its ability to minimize the disruption caused by peak stadium traffic. This requires careful planning and a willingness on the part of professional sports teams to be good citizens. The political power that professional sports teams currently wield forces neighborhood businesses and residents to shoulder a disproportionate share of the risks and inconvenience associated with the influx of fans on game days. Local residents, business employees, and other business patrons have to be given parking priorities. Remote parking and an emphasis on public transportation are essential to maintaining neighborhood economic vitality.

In addition to parking concessions, owners of professional sports teams need to share the commerce associated with sports spectating. The modern stadium doubles as a shopping mall complete with food courts whose operation serves to minimize the neighborhood economic impact. The fact that souvenir venders are prohibited from operating too close to some new stadiums in the U.S. is one overt manifestation of excessive team influence and a lack of citizenship.

Legislators have been sensitive to the demise of urban America for a variety of reasons, and, as a consequence, initiatives designed to rejuvenate downtowns have enjoyed some support at the state and federal levels. There are what economists would identify as externality issues associated with urban blight, and it could be argued that revitalizing downtowns generates benefits that spill beyond the urban core. If this is so, nonlocal public subsidies for downtown redevelopment may have merit. Before stadiums can be used to rejuvenate the downtown, it must be determined that they represent the best use of that land. Parking and the nature of economic development that sports fosters are factors that have to be weighed in those land-use decisions. Professional sports leagues operate as unregulated monopolies, and until that issue is addressed, poor decisions with regard to the location and operation of stadiums will continue to occur. The most important policy implication is to revamp the structure of professional sports leagues to ensure that the greatest good for the greatest number is ensured.

Notes

1. Direct expenditures are "multiplied" by a number that represents the respending of dollars spent as a consequence of the sports event. For example, the waiters at a restaurant that attracts fans after the game receives tips that are in turn spent by the waiter on goods and services provided by the local economy. For an example of an analysis that uses gross expenditures see Shils (1989).
2. With the construction of the baseball stadium, approximately 1,200 of those parking spots have been eliminated in the south parking lot. For an event that attracts a capacity crowd, the 2,400 available stadium parking spaces implies there are 27 fans for each parking space. Given the use of automobiles by fans, the industry standard has been three or four fans for each parking space.
3. Representing the neighborhood as a business admittedly captures only a portion of a community's character and quality of life, but such a representation provides some useful insights.
4. In the July 24, 1998 survey conducted by krs services, inc., businesses gave parking the highest priority in improving Pioneer Square. Parking, however, is not a problem unique to Pioneer Square. In six other recently surveyed Seattle business districts, parking was listed as the first or second highest priority in four of the six districts.

APPENDIX

Survey of the Effects the Kingdome on Commercial Activity in Seattle

Note to the participant: Your responses to this survey will be kept strictly confidential. Individual responses will not be reported separately. The data a business provides will be reported only as part of an overall result in which variables such as the change in revenues will be represented as percent changes.

1. Business or firm name_____

2. Location of business _____

3. Proximity to Kingdome_____walking minutes_____miles

4. Type of business _____
   (Office use only: SIC code =   ).

5. Business structure: ___ Corporate ___Franchise ___ Sole proprietorship
   ___ Locally owned ___ Nationally owned

6. On-street parking ___Yes ___No
   Parking on street is metered ___Yes ___No
   ___ Distance to nearest parking garage/lot
   ___ Proximity to public transportation.

7. Revenue generated by your business on game day/night for the Mariners
   ___ increases by more than 25% ___ increases by less than 25%
   ___ decreases by more than 25% ___ decreases by less than 25%
   ___ stays the same

8. Revenue generated by your business on game day/night for the Seahawks
   ___ increases by more than 25% ___ increases by less than 25%
   ___ decreases by more than 25% ___ decreases by less than 25%
   ___ stays the same

9. If revenue decreases on game day it is because of (rank on a scale of 0–5, where 0 represents no effect and 5 represents a significant effect):
___ inadequate parking ___ competition from stadium amenities
___ general stadium congestion ___ behavior of those who attend games.

10. Revenue Data:
Typical revenue from the business: ___ Weekday ___Weekend
Typical revenue from the business during a Mariners' game:
___ Weekday ___ Weekend
Typical revenue from the business during a Seahawks' game:
___ Weekday ___ Weekend

11. Other comments:

References

Austrian, Ziona, and Mark Rosentraub. 1997. "Cleveland's Gateway to the Future." In *Sports, Jobs & Taxes: The Economic Impact of Sports Teams and Stadiums*, Roger G. Noll and Andrew Zimbalist, eds. Washington, D.C.: The Brookings Institution Press, pp. 355–384.

Baade, Robert A. 1996. "Professional Sports as Catalysts for Metropolitan Economic Development." *Journal of Urban Affairs* 18(1): 1–17.

Baade, Robert A., and Allen R. Sanderson. 1997. "The Employment Effect of Teams and Sports Facilities." In *Sports, Jobs & Taxes: The Economic Impact of Sports Teams and Stadiums*, Roger G. Noll and Andrew Zimbalist, eds. Washington, D.C.: The Brookings Institution Press, pp. 92–118.

Conway, R.S., and W.B. Byers. 1994. "Seattle Mariners Baseball Club Economic Impact." Photocopy. August.

Hamilton, Bruce W., and Peter Kahn. 1997. "Baltimore's Camden Yards Ballparks." In *Sports, Jobs & Taxes: The Economic Impact of Sports Teams and Stadiums*, Roger G. Noll and Andrew Zimbalist, eds. Washington, D.C.: The Brookings Institution Press, pp. 245–281.

krs services, inc., The Russell Group. 1998. "Pioneer Square Business Surveys: Initial Findings." Photocopy (draft), July 24.

Lowry, Philip J. 1992. *Green Cathedrals*. Reading, Massachusetts: Addison-Wesley Publishing Co., Inc.

Noll, Roger G., and Andrew Zimbalist. 1997. "The Economic Impact of Sports Teams and Facilities." In *Sports, Jobs & Taxes: The Economic Impact of Sports Teams and Stadiums*, Roger G. Noll and Andrew Zimbalist, eds. Washington, D.C.: The Brookings Institution Press, pp. 55–91.

Shils, Edward. 1989. "Report to the Philadelphia Professional Sports Consortium on Its Contribution to the Economy of Philadelphia During 1988." Photocopy. December 4.

3

Who is Sitting in the Stands?
The Income Levels of Sports Fans

John J. Siegfried and Timothy Peterson
Vanderbilt University

About a decade ago, an unprecedented professional sports stadium and arena construction boom emerged in the United States as professional sports team owners began to recognize their ability to play image-conscious metropolitan areas off against each other. New stadiums and arenas were attractive to these team owners not because their games could not be played in existing facilities—most of the existing stadiums and arenas were less than thirty years old and many were far from sold out—but rather because revenue prospects began to depend on new stadium configurations. Architects of the 1960s and 1970s who built the old-style arenas and stadiums did not anticipate how many wealthy individuals and corporations would be willing to pay for the status, exclusivity, and amenities of club seats and luxury boxes. However, rapid economic growth, rising income inequality, and the increasing popularity of relative status have combined to create an enormous demand for high-end sports services in the 1990s. When team owners report that their stadium is "inadequate," they mean that it is inadequate to produce the revenues that the team owner would prefer to collect.

Revenue enhancement alone, however, is not necessarily worthwhile to team owners. Prospective incremental revenues must be weighed against the additional costs required to attract them. That is where a taxpayer-financed stadium fits into a team's income statement. Stadiums that provide exclusive seating in luxury boxes and club seats are expensive to build. Costs are always lower, of course, if the owner can get someone else to foot the construction bill and then pay them a trivial rental rate for use of the facility, as characterizes many recently constructed sports stadiums and arenas.[1] Furthermore, without the sunk costs of stadium ownership to tie him down, the owner increases his ability to extract further concessions from the local population by periodically threatening to move the team. If the team receives revenues from nonsports uses of the facility throughout the year, a contract provision that is fashionable in modern stadium and arena leases, the owners' revenues can be expanded further.

The vast majority of premier league professional sports stadiums constructed in the 1990s have been financed partly by taxpayers, including federal, state, and local (Noll and Zimbalist 1998, appendix to chapter 1). About 25 state and local governments have provided at least $100 million each in subsidies to professional sports teams (Rosentraub 1997, pp. 16). Even the few new stadiums that have been privately financed usually have benefited from a substantial public underwriting for access roads and utilities infrastructure.

Federal taxpayers contribute to these stadiums and arenas primarily by means of the federal government forgoing tax revenue on interest paid to holders of tax exempt municipal bonds used to finance construction (Zimmerman 1998). These forgone tax revenues must either be made up elsewhere or public services reduced accordingly. State and local tax support is more direct, often involving direct outlays of property tax receipts, or the earmarking of either sales tax revenues collected on tickets to the events held in the facility or revenues from a lottery. Unless all of the facility's patrons are from outside the local area, at least some, and usually a large proportion of these earmarked tax revenues would have been collected by the state or local tax authority anyway as local consumers purchased other taxable items as part of their established expenditure pattern.

In spite of the often emotional public debate about the equity consequences of public policy, the controversy surrounding stadiums and arenas has focused largely on local economic development prospects and opportunities to enhance a metropolitan area's public image. Unfortunately, the debates usually center on the financing of stadiums and arenas rather than on net economic effects. Financial transfers are treated as costs to those who provide the financing and benefits to those who receive it regardless of the expansion or contraction of real economic activity. The focus on financial implications of public subsidies for sports facilities leaves both the efficiency and equity consequences of such policies largely unexamined.

EVALUATING PUBLIC PROJECTS

In the 1960s economists adopted a taxonomy for evaluating public projects. This taxonomy involved two parts: efficiency and equity effects (Okun 1975). A literature developed to assist in measuring economic benefits and costs and especially in identifying easy to overlook opportunity costs. Methodological contributions focused on properly weighing benefits against costs.

In recent years economists have begun to apply this taxonomy to the public provision of sports facilities. Robert Baade (1987, 1994, 1996) stimulated more careful analysis of the claims of stadium proponents through a series of studies assessing the economic impact of new teams and/or facilities on local economies. Roger Noll and Andrew Zimbalist's (1997) recently published *Sports, Jobs, and Taxes* organizes much of what is now known about the efficiency consequences of publicly provided stadiums and arenas and helps to distinguish real economic effects of such facilities from the financial transfers surrounding them.

EQUITY ISSUES

To date, however, there seems to have been little interest in the equity consequences of public policy relating to sports facilities. Some groups that oppose political referendums on public subsidies for sports stadiums or arenas assert that the poor are buying playgrounds for the rich, but there is little objective evidence available about the income redistribution consequences that arise when communities allocate public funds for the construction of sports facilities for privately owned professional sports teams.[2]

The distributional consequences of public projects are complicated because many direct burdens and benefits are passed along to taxpayers or beneficiaries who do not attract attention. The extent to which benefits and/or costs are passed along depends on the magnitude of various elasticities of supply and demand that are extremely difficult to evaluate. For example, a common method of financing new venues is to earmark either sales taxes collected on tickets sold to events in the facility, on restaurants, on rental cars, or on hotel and motel use. Even if one assumes that none of these taxes would have been collected by the taxing authority were those who buy tickets to have purchased alternative items, the ultimate incidence of such ad valorem sales or hotel taxes depends on the elasticities of supply and demand. As thousands of introductory economics students show on problem sets and exams each year, if demand is inelastic and supply is elastic, the consumers bear relatively more of the burden. On the other hand, if demand is elastic, and supply is inelastic, the suppliers bear most of the burden. The challenge, of course, is measuring the relevant elasticities.

WHO PAYS THE SUBSIDY?

A careful accounting of the distributional effects of publicly subsidized stadium or arena projects requires an assessment of the sources of revenue as well as the beneficiaries of the services provided and the recipients of the revenues. Identifying who pays for stadium subsidies is complicated because there are usually multiple revenue sources, and the ultimate incidence of different taxes varies. Local taxes are raised primarily via levies on retail sales, property, and hotel and motel use. Because the marginal propensity to consume is less than one, general sales taxes are usually considered regressive, especially if the tax base includes food and clothing. Property taxes, at least in intermediate ranges, are thought by some economists (Pechman 1985) to be proportional; at the higher ranges they may be progressive (O'Sullivan 1996). The incidence of hotel and motel taxes is difficult to assess because such taxes are paid primarily by myriad businesses that, in competitive markets, would pass them along to their customers. Incidence would ultimately depend on the affluence of those customers. In an analysis that tried to trace such specific taxes through the economy to the individuals who ultimately pay them, Siegfried, McElroy, and Sweeney (1982) found hotel and motel taxes to be progressive.

State revenues to subsidize sports facilities are raised primarily from general sales taxes, personal and corporate income taxes, lotteries, or a "sin tax" on alcohol. Both federal, and state or local personal income taxes are modestly progressive (Clotfelter and Cook 1989, p. 227). The incidence of corporate income taxes is complex and remains controversial. Lotteries are regressive, although they may be less objectionable because they are a "voluntary tax" (Clotfelter and Cook 1989, p. 223). Siegfried and colleagues found taxes on alcohol to be mildly progressive; Clotfelter and Cook (p. 227) report evidence that taxes on alcohol are regressive.

Finally, the federal government's revenue sources are so diverse that it would be virtually impossible to predict which taxes would be higher because of federal subsidies to sports facilities. Because federally tax exempt municipal bonds are attractive only to those lenders in relatively high marginal income tax brackets, however, we can be sure that some of the benefits accrue to relatively high income individuals. The costs are borne either by those who would have benefited from the alternative public projects that would have been funded in the absence of the tax break for municipal bonds used to finance sports facilities or by those who pay the marginal taxes.

WHO BENEFITS DIRECTLY FROM THE SUBSIDY?

The incidence of taxation is a subject for another day, however. Here we want to learn about the income characteristics of the beneficiaries of publicly provided sports facilities. This is but a simple first step toward assessing the distributional impact of public subsidies for professional sports facilities. To address this question, it is useful first to categorize the primary beneficiaries of subsidies for new sports stadiums or arenas.

The most obvious beneficiaries are claimants on team revenues. New sports stadiums are desired by teams because they enhance team revenues through opportunities to lease luxury boxes, sell club seating tickets at premium prices, increase concession revenues, and expand advertising revenues, e.g., signs in the stadium and/or stadium "naming rights." To the extent that new playing facilities increase the demand for tickets, owners of teams in other league cities benefit too through revenue sharing in Major League Baseball (MLB) and in the National Football League (NFL). Net revenues also climb as a team's facility costs disappear. Players and team owners carve up most of professional sports teams' revenues. Both groups are comprised of very high income individuals. There is little doubt that to the extent that public subsidies of sports stadiums and arenas allow teams to increase net revenues by expanding revenue opportunities and reducing team costs, the lion's share of those revenues go to individuals in the top one-tenth of one percent of the national income distribution.

Of the 115 major league men's professional sports teams operating in 1998, the controlling interest in at least 28 was owned by an individual on the 1998 *Forbes* magazine list of the wealthiest 400 Americans (Gorham, Kafka, and Neelakantan 1998). If the 50 wealthiest family groups and minority interests in sports teams are added to the number of teams owned by "top 400" wealthiest individuals, the count swells to 38.[3] Public subsidies to stadiums or arenas constitute a subsidy program for some of the wealthiest people in the country, each of whom has net assets exceeding half a billion dollars.

Players are not nearly as wealthy as owners. The average income of players in the National Basketball Association (NBA), National Hockey League (NHL), NFL, and MLB in 1998 was $2.6, $1.2, $0.8, and $1.3 million, respectively; minimum salaries in the leagues were $242,000, $125,000, $158,000, and $170,000, respectively. While not in the stratosphere of the average team owner's wealth, even those premier league professional athletes earning the "minimum wage" earn numerous standard deviations of income more than typical Americans. Those athletes who are paid the average for their league earn more in a single year than an average American might expect to earn in a lifetime.

Team owners and players receive most of a team's incremental revenues because they own the ultimate scarce resources. Team owners possess the scarce rights to participate in the premier league in their sport. They limit entry into the league to preserve this scarcity value. Absent scarcity of franchises, there would be little reason for anyone to pay much of anything in excess of the market value of future player contracts (the relatively small extent to which the value of the players' services exceeds their contractual salaries) and equipment for an existing franchise when they could simply secure a new one. Since expansion franchises have no player contracts or equipment, they would be free. The actual price of franchises reflects monopoly power and little else. Owners clearly have title to a scarce resource—access to the premier league championship.

Players also possess monopoly rights, since they (and especially "star" players) own the scarce resources necessary to produce professional sporting events. Fans would not be willing to pay to see Tim Peterson and John Siegfried replace Michael Jordan and Scottie Pippen on the NBA champion Chicago Bulls. In fact, fans would not be willing to pay as much to see top NBA "lottery" draft picks replace Jordan and Pippen. Star players control a differentiated product for which there are often no good substitutes in the eyes of the fans—their athletic talent and personalities. Under such circumstances economic theory predicts that at least some portion of net revenues made available by a public subsidy that expands gross revenues and reduces facility costs will be transferred to players.[4] These net revenues are virtually all economic rent.

In addition to the revenues divided between players and owners, there may be direct benefits that accrue to consumers. Only in that rare case when a consumer is completely indifferent to the choice between purchasing a good or service or not is no consumer's surplus created. In recent years, sports teams have successfully designed price discrimination schemes to extract some of this consumer's surplus. However, because few people agonize over the decisions either to buy a ticket or to watch a game on television, there is no question that some surplus remains for almost every purchaser of tickets or viewer of games on television.

The direct demand for professional sporting events is manifested primarily through the demand for tickets to live professional sporting events and the demand for viewing games on television. Although there is no way to determine the magnitude of consumer surplus enjoyed by those who buy tickets or view games on television, we can be sure that most of the fans receive <u>some</u> consumer surplus. It is of more than passing interest to identify these individuals because they are the local consumers who will enjoy increased utility from a subsidy to a stadium or arena that either prevents a team from moving elsewhere or lures a team into the area.[5] Because there is little question that the owners and players are relatively affluent, the only prospective <u>direct</u> beneficiaries of public sports facility subsidies who are not wealthy are the fans.

INDIRECT BENEFITS

The objective of this essay is to identify the income distribution position of the direct consumers of sports. In addition to direct private benefits manifested in consumer's surplus, some indirect "public consumption" benefit is likely to be provided by sports stadiums or arenas. Such external benefits may arise from increased self-esteem enjoyed by residents who believe that they are better off living in a "big league city," or who at least believe that their lives are enhanced if others view their community as a "major league place" (Rosentraub 1997, pp. 25–26). The fact that virtually all well- conducted studies of the economic development effects of professional sports teams and/or new stadiums or arenas find no impact whatsoever (an exception being a recent study by Coats and Humphreys [1999], who found a negative effect) does not undermine the possibility of external benefits, although it casts doubt on their magnitude. Trickle-down economic impacts are not the only source of external benefits. So long as the local residents <u>believe</u> that they are better off with an enhanced public image and we respect consumer sovereignty, then they benefit from the team, stadium, or arena whether the basis for their belief is valid or not.

External benefits can also arise from the personal consumption of following a team's fortunes, discussing the team's success around the water cooler, or as a rallying point that brings a community together. Of course external costs may also arise from depression caused by a team that chronically loses, increased traffic congestion on game days, domestic conflict generated by the home team's game being televised during Thanksgiving dinner, or time diverted from work effort as employees congregate around the water cooler more frequently than their supervisor would like.

It is difficult to determine how such external benefits might be distributed across individuals at different points along the income distribution. Before we even worry about their distribution, however, we need to document the existence and magnitude of external benefits. While doing so, we should also catalog any external costs associated with the presence of a professional sports team. Zimmerman (1998, p. 122) suggests that these benefits might be valued equally by all individuals or that fans (particularly those fans who purchase tickets to games) are likely to value them more than others. If such external benefits are distributed in proportion to fan purchases of tickets, then our efforts to understand the income position of those who purchase tickets and view games on television will simultaneously reveal the distribution of the external benefits. On the other hand, the distribution of these external benefits may differ from the distribution of benefits that accrue to buyers of tickets and viewers of televised game broadcasts.

WHO BUYS THE TICKETS TO SPORTING EVENTS?

The individuals who purchase tickets for professional sporting events are the people who enjoy the consumers' surplus from the direct consumption of sporting event services. Thus, it is of interest to learn precisely who are the people who enjoy benefits in excess of the price they pay for tickets to the games. It is these people who secure direct benefits from the presence of a professional sporting team and/or stadium or arena. To the extent that a publicly subsidized stadium or arena attracts a team to a community or prevents an incumbent franchise from moving elsewhere, it is those who buy tickets to the games or who receive more enjoyment from watching games on television that involve their hometown team rather than teams from other cities who are direct beneficiaries of the public subsidy.

Our argument that fans benefit from a publicly subsidized stadium is not a claim that ticket prices are lower because of the public subsidy. Indeed, as a reduction in fixed costs, a rent subsidy imbedded in a 25- or 30-year lease is unlikely to affect ticket prices at all. Rather it is a balancing of marginal costs against marginal revenues that identifies the profit maximizing ticket price level. Our interest in the affluence of sports ticket purchasers instead hinges on the belief that the very exist-ence of the opportunity to purchase tickets and attend games in one's hometown depends on the public subsidy because of the artificial scar-city of premier league teams created by the monopoly leagues. The public subsidy creates some amount of consumer surplus for the fans who purchase tickets by means of its responsibility for the team's pres-ence. Each fan who purchases tickets must be better off than he or she would have been in the absence of the team, otherwise they would sim-ply continue their previous consumption pattern and decline to pur-chase tickets.

THE DATA

As part of its Consumer Expenditure Survey (CES), the Bureau of Labor Statistics interviews a continuous rotating panel of households in the U.S. to collect data for calculating the Consumer Price Index. This nationally representative recall survey provides information on expenditure patterns and income levels of slightly more than 5,000 households each quarter.[6] It is constructed so that each quarter can be treated as an independent sample; thus four quarters of data furnishes a sample of about 20,000 U.S. households.

We use two types of information from the 1994 CES samples: pre-tax family income and itemized expenditures for: "admission fees to sporting events," and "admission fees to sporting events on out-of-town trips." Admission fees include both single-game and season tickets. All of the sporting event tickets documented in the CES were pur-chased by individuals; we have no information on tickets purchased by businesses or who enjoys the use of those tickets. It is likely that this omission biases downward the reported income levels of those who attend sporting events.

Sporting events are all inclusive. They range from auto and horse racing to professional golf and tennis, or whatever survey respondents consider "sporting events." Minor league baseball as well as college sporting events are included. A large fraction of the money spent on tickets, however, is accounted for by the four major men's professional team sports—baseball, basketball, football, and ice hockey, each of which is well practiced in the art of negotiating subsidized facilities for their team's games.[7]

Data from the 1972–1973 CES, revealed that the typical purchasers of season tickets to sporting events had median incomes 58 percent above the average (McElroy, Siegfried, and Sweeney 1982). Those purchasers of single-game tickets had median incomes about 10 percent above the overall average. In the early 1970s, sports teams had not yet discovered the lucrative personal seat license (PSL) system of extracting payments in excess of the face value of tickets from more-rabid fans. The price of PSLs makes it unlikely that a stadium crowd in 2000 consists of many people holding minimum wage jobs, aside from the ushers and concession workers serving those in the club seats and luxury boxes. If anything, the disparity between the income level of those attending professional sporting events and the average "Joe Six-pack" has widened over time.

By 1994 the CES no longer separated season tickets from single-game tickets. It did, however, distinguish tickets purchased while at home from those purchased while traveling out-of-town. We combine these two categories of sporting event tickets into a single "sporting event tickets" category.[8]

Our analysis is based on four quarters of data from 1994. Tickets to sporting events were purchased by an average of 5.6 percent of the consumer units each quarter (totaling 1,147 consumer units for the year). Thus, up to (but more likely a lot less than) 22 percent of consumer units might purchase tickets during a full year.

INCOME LEVELS OF SPORTS TICKET PURCHASERS

Table 1 reports measures of central tendency for income levels of consumers who do and do not purchase sporting event tickets. The unweighted mean personal income level of consumers who bought sporting event tickets shows that they enjoy average incomes 59 percent above those who do not purchase sporting event tickets.[9] The weighted mean weights the income levels of households that bought tickets by their expenditures on tickets and is a more accurate reflection of the personal income levels of those who typically use the tickets.

Table 1 Income Levels of Consumers by Attendance at Sporting Events, 1994[a]

Income of	Simple mean	Weighted mean	Median
A. Consumers who purchase tickets to sporting events	$48,288	$56,124	$42,663
B. Consumers who do not purchase tickets to sporting events	$30,350	$30,350	$22,258
C. Ratio of A:B	1.59	1.85	1.92

SOURCE: Consumer Expenditure Survey, 1994 (Bureau of Labor Statistics).
[a] Incomes are in nominal 1994 dollars.

Not surprisingly, the weighted mean shows a larger income gap (85 percent) between consumers who do and do not purchase tickets to sporting events. We also report median income levels because mean income levels can be affected by extremely high incomes of a few consumers and by the 1994 CES practice of "topcoding" all incomes exceeding $300,000 at $300,000.[10] Using medians, the difference between the two groups is 92 percent.

Depending on the measure of central tendency, sporting event consumers have incomes from 59 to 92 percent above the levels of consumers who do not buy sporting event tickets. When consumers who buy sporting event tickets are mixed with those who do not, the 1994 median income level is $23,194. Thus, the median income level of consumers of sporting event tickets is 84 percent above the overall median income level. This number is in contrast to the 58 percent differential for season tickets and 10 percent differential for single-game tickets in 1972–1973. Because only a small fraction of the consumer units purchase tickets, the reported averages for those who buy no tickets at all are always close to the overall U.S. average income.

In computing weighted means, those consumers purchasing a disproportionate share of tickets to sporting events have a greater effect on the average income level. The small sample size of 1,147 consumer units that purchased sporting event tickets risks placing undue reliance on the consumption patterns of relatively few consumers. To assess the sensitivity of our results to this possibility, we eliminate households that individually account for over 5 percent of the total expenditures for sporting event tickets in a quarter. This criterion eliminates seven households (two low-income and five high-income), after which the weighted-mean income of consumers of sporting event tickets drops from $56,124 to $55,883. This still exceeds the mean income of consumers who did not purchase any sporting event tickets by 84 percent.

To maintain individual respondent confidentiality, the CES topcoded income at $300,000 in 1994. Four percent of households that purchased sporting event tickets were topcoded in contrast to 1.6 percent of households that did not purchase sporting event tickets. Topcoding causes a greater downward bias in the income level of consumers of sporting event tickets than in the income levels of consumers who do not buy sporting event tickets. It thus causes our calculations to understate the differences in income levels between sports consumers and others. Topcoding also reveals that sporting event tickets are more than twice as likely to be purchased by consumers with income exceeding $300,000 as are other goods and services.

The conclusion is clear. Incomes of consumers who purchase sporting event tickets are significantly greater than incomes of consumers who do not buy tickets to sporting events. If we were able to include in the analysis individuals who enjoy access to tickets purchased by small businesses and corporations and those who have leased luxury boxes, the difference surely would be even greater. Ticket prices to minor league contests and college games are substantially lower than ticket prices to premier league professional games. Because our analysis combines all of these types of events, it undoubtedly understates the income gap between those who attend major league professional sporting events and the general public. As more new stadiums with relatively more luxury boxes and club seats are completed, the gap will continue to grow.

INDIRECT EVIDENCE FROM TARGETED ADVERTISING

Consumer Expenditure Survey data do not identify the particular sports events for which tickets are purchased. To explore differences in income levels among the fans of different sports and to assess the reasonableness of our CES-based estimates, we collected information about advertising in event programs, in stadiums and arenas, and on televised broadcasts of games. Advertising in event programs is directed at individuals who attend the events. Advertising on televised broadcasts is directed at people who watch the games on television. Advertising in the facility is directed at both groups, as those who attend the games see signage in the stadium or arena, and those who watch on television may see the signage too.

Advertising in event programs thus provides information that should match the information we collected from the CES. Our analysis of income levels of consumers based on advertising assumes that advertisers direct their messages at people who are most likely to purchase their products. We expect to find that the products purchased frequently by sports fans who buy tickets are advertised in event programs. Products that are likely to be purchased by sports fans who view games on television are likely to be advertised during television commercials. By looking at the income levels of the consumers of these products, we can infer the income levels of those who attend games and those who view them on television.[11]

To assess the income levels of the consumers of the various goods and services targeted by each advertising type, we first classify the specific product advertised and then identify the median income of all consumers of that product from the CES. If an advertiser sells products in various CES categories, we assign the advertisement to all of those categories and average the median incomes of consumers of products in the various categories to create a representative income level for the target audience of the advertisement. We aggregate the income levels across the various products advertised via a particular medium (e.g., event program or signage or television) for each of the four professional team sports by calculating the median of the median incomes of consumers of the various advertised products. The procedure is illustrated in Table 2, which reports the advertisers in a randomly selected Baltimore Orioles baseball game program and the respective median income levels of the consumers of the products sold by the advertisers.

Our research assignment consisted of reviewing many spectator programs, advertisements on stadium walls and scoreboards, and viewing over 30 televised games. The latter was accomplished by videotap-

Table 2 Baltimore Orioles Program Advertisements with Corresponding Median Income Level of Consumers of the Products or Services Advertised

Products or services advertised	Median income levels of consumers of product or service based on CES ($)
Bacardi rum	23,480
Rums of Puerto Rico	23,480
Beck's beer	23,480
Gordon's vodka	23,480
Super Pretzel	25,000
Lemon Chill	25,000
Esskay hot-dogs	25,000
Old El Paso (food)	25,000
Sprint (telephone service)	25.781
Coca-Cola	27,979
Milk	27,979
Powerade (sports drink)	27,979
Deer Park (bottled water)	27,979
Rawlings Sporting Goods	28,110
Energizer batteries	29,820
Value City Furniture	31,213
Bravo Card (ATM card)	31,425
Matrix (hair care)	33,801
State Farm Insurance	34,000
NationsBank	34,125
First Union Bank	34,125
First National Bank	34,125
J.C. Penney (department store)	37,000
Montgomery Ward (department store)	37,000
St. Agnes Healthcare	37,850
Sheraton Inner Harbor Hotel	37,895
Motorola (electronics)	41,091
Adventure World (amusement park)	41,161

Table 2 (continued)

Products or services advertised	Median income levels of consumers of product or service based on CES ($)
Sharp computers/electronics	41,610
Starter sportswear	41,610
Diamond sportswear	41,610
Southwest Airlines	42,000
MasterCard	44,813
Saturn	48,704
Trane air conditioning	49,313
Office Depot	50,175
Tuxedo House (tuxedo rental)	52,215
Cellular One	67,018
Median of the median incomes of consumers of products advertised	37,063

ing the games and reviewing the tapes.[12] The peculiar twist to our research is that we fast-forwarded through the games and watched the advertisements at normal speed!

There are some inherent weaknesses in this approach. First, products often are differentiated to appeal to people of different means. The CES does not distinguish product categories in terms of the income of the target audiences, however. There is no separation of "restaurants for high-income people" from "restaurants for low-income people." Premium brands of imported beer are lumped in with local generic beers. Because we group together differentiated products targeted at low- and high-income consumers, our advertising-based method of estimating consumer income levels should reveal less divergence between the income levels of sports consumers and the income levels of nonsports consumers than actually exists.

A second problem is securing sufficient data. In several cases, our sample sizes are sufficiently small that the evidence is anecdotal rather than systematic. We are missing signage information for basketball and television broadcasting information for football. We report medians to

Table 3 Consumer Income Levels by Sports Advertising Targets[a]

Sport	Event programs			Facility signs			Television advertising		
	Income ($)	N	Ratio[b]	Income ($)	N	Ratio[b]	Income ($)	N	Ratio[b]
Baseball	31,898	10	1.43	33,391	9	1.50	36,277	20	1.63
Basketball	39,075	2	1.76	n/a[c]	n/a	n/a	40,711	8	1.83
Football	38,189	6	1.72	29,682	3	1.33	n/a	n/a	n/a
Ice hockey	40,255	2	1.81	37,642	6	1.69	37,065	4	1.66
Mean of medians across all sports	37,326			33,572			38,016		
Median income of households that do not purchase tickets to sporting events	22,258			22,258			22,258		

SOURCE: Authors' survey and Consumer Expenditure Survey, 1994 (Bureau of Labor Statistics).

[a] Incomes are in nominal 1994 dollars.

[b] Ratio is the ratio of the respective income levels to the income levels of consumer units that do not purchase tickets to sporting events.

[c] n/a indicates that no data were collected.

avoid distortions caused by topcoding incomes. Although the advertisements were run in 1997, the median income levels we assign to the products are from the 1994 CES. Thus the income data are in 1994 nominal dollars. All of the estimates based on the targets of advertising are reported in Table 3.

EVENT PROGRAMS

We assembled randomly selected game programs from 10 major league baseball teams, seven professional football teams, two professional basketball franchises, and two professional ice hockey teams. The median of the median income levels of consumers of the various products advertised in baseball programs ranged from $27,980 at Philadelphia Phillies games to $38,500 for those of the Chicago White Sox games. The mean over 10 sampled baseball teams was $31,898.

The corresponding median income level targeted for fans of the seven football teams ranged from $35,000 for Seattle Seahawks fans to $40,225 for those of the Chicago Bears. In basketball, the Indiana Pacers had a targeted median income level of $37,895; the Minnesota Timberwolves, $40,255. Both ice hockey teams in the sample (the Detroit Red Wings and the Tampa Bay Lightning) had identical median incomes of consumers of products advertised in their program of $40,255.

The ratio of the estimated income levels of consumers of products advertised in game programs to the income levels of consumers who do not purchase tickets to sporting events (from the CES) is also reported in Table 3. It ranges from 1.43 for baseball to 1.81 for ice hockey. The ratios for basketball, football, and ice hockey, ranging from 1.72 to 1.81, are relatively close to the comparable ratio of 1.92 based on the CES data on sports event ticket purchases. This is especially so in light of our expectation that the advertising-based estimates would understate the gap in income levels between sports ticket purchasers and others.[13] The ratio for baseball is noticeably lower than for the other three sports. Perhaps this is because the lowest-priced tickets for baseball games are substantially below the lowest-priced tickets for the other three sports thereby attracting a different clientele to games.

STADIUM OR ARENA SIGNS

Stadium signs are directed both at people who attend the live events and at the television audience. A similar procedure was used to compute median incomes for the targeted consumers of stadium or arena advertisements for each team in our sample. These incomes were then averaged over the teams and are reported in Table 3.

The median income of the consumers targeted by signage ranges from $28,010 at Los Angeles Dodgers games to $38,500 at Florida Marlins games. For the eight baseball teams common to the sample, the simple correlation between the estimated income levels of advertising targets of event programs and those using stadium signage is +0.36. The medians for the three football teams range from $26,808 for the Buffalo Bills to $34,126 for the Oakland Raiders; and for the six ice hockey teams from $35,000 for the Detroit Red Wings to $39,000 for the Colorado Avalanche.

In contrast to event programs, which are targeted only at people who attend games, football stadium and ice hockey arena signs appear to target lower-income consumers who may be viewing televised broadcasts. The income levels of those targeted for baseball signage, however, do not differ much from those targeted by baseball event program advertising. This inconsistency may reflect the inaccessibility of football and ice hockey event tickets to lower income consumers who, therefore, substitute television viewing for live attendance. However, the income levels of fans who attend baseball games and those who watch them on television diverge less, perhaps because baseball consumers generally have access to lower-priced bleacher seats.

TELEVISION ADVERTISEMENTS

Because television commercials are directed at those who are not attending the events in person, we might expect to observe a continuation of the income-level trends that became apparent as we moved from event programs to facility signage. To assess these income levels, we recorded all of the advertisements on 32 nationally broadcast games. The sample includes 20 baseball games, eight basketball games, and four ice hockey games. Because the teams varied and the games were broadcast nationally, we do not distinguish income levels by teams.

Only ice hockey advertising follows the expected trend of targeting lower-income fans for products advertised on televised games than for products advertised in event programs, and then only modestly so.[14] We find little difference between the median income of the consumers targeted in televised basketball advertising and that of consumers targeted in basketball game programs. In baseball, the median income of targeted consumers of products touted on televised broadcasts actually exceeds the median income of consumers targeted in game programs. If anything is to be learned from the differences, it is that fans of football and ice hockey are split by income level, with the more affluent viewing games in person. For baseball, the opposite appears to be true; and for basketball, there is no discernible difference in income levels of fans sitting in the arena and those sitting on the couch watching television. The median income level of consumer units targeted on all sports television broadcasts is similar, ranging from 63 percent to 83 percent above the income levels of consumers who do not purchase tickets to sporting events. Thus it appears that television viewers of sporting events have incomes modestly below those fans who attend the games but are still relatively affluent.

Patterns of household access to televised sporting events undoubtedly contribute to the affluence level of television viewers. The percentage of individuals who watch some television does not vary much by household income level (ranging from 91 percent for households with income levels less than $10,000 annually to 92 percent for households with income levels between $20,000 and $30,000 to 89 percent for households with income levels exceeding $50,000 in 1996). However, the percentage of individuals who view cable television does vary substantially by household income level, from 42 percent for households with income levels less than $10,000 annually to 58 percent for households with income levels between $20,000 and $30,000, to 74 percent for households with income levels exceeding $50,000 in 1996 (*Statistical Abstract of the United States* 1996, p. 561). A considerable proportion of televised sporting events is distributed exclusively on cable television, including, but not limited to, ESPN and ESPN2.

CONCLUSION

Consumers of sporting event tickets enjoy incomes substantially above the average. Although consumers who watch games on television appear to have lower incomes, they too are affluent in comparison with the nation's overall average income.

A careful documentation of the redistributional effects of public subsidies for sports facilities requires an accounting of the distribution of the subsidies to the teams (which are generally divided between players and owners, almost all individuals in both groups being very affluent), an assessment of the incidence of indirect benefits such as community image enhancement or the enjoyment of "following the local team," and an evaluation of the incidence of the funding mechanisms (taxes and lotteries) used to raise the revenue. One portion of the redistribution—the consumers' surplus flowing to fans—seems to favor relatively more affluent individuals. The remaining aspects of the redistribution are easier to assess intuitively and support speculation that the public funding of sports facilities redistributes wealth from individuals with lower and middle incomes to those with much higher incomes. Whether this redistribution is desirable or not, depends on one's views about its fairness and about the assessment of other economic effects of publicly funded stadiums and arenas.

Notes

Siegfried is Professor of Economics at Vanderbilt University. Peterson earned Honors in Economics and graduated with a B.A. from Vanderbilt University in 1998. T. Aldrich Finegan, Malcolm Getz, Allen Sanderson, and Andrew Zimbalist provided helpful comments on an earlier draft.

1. The desired size and amenities of a stadium are also affected by its financing. As the team's share of incremental construction cost declines, it will elect a larger and better outfitted facility.
2. A notable exception is Zimmerman's (1998) analysis of the distributional consequences of the federal tax exemption for municipal bonds.
3. This count does not include indirect team ownership such as Rupert Murdoch's News Corporation's ownership of the Los Angeles Dodgers.
4. In several of the sports leagues (e.g., NFL, NBA) players share added revenues with owners on the basis of formulas instituted in conjunction with payroll ceilings that were negotiated between owners and the players' union.

5. The relevant net gain to sports ticket buyers is the <u>difference</u> between the consumers' surplus they enjoy from the opportunity to purchase tickets and what they would have received from buying the goods and services that would have been purchased by them were the sporting event tickets not available.
6. About one-fifth of the sample is replaced by new households each quarter so that after five quarters the entire sample has turned over.
7. Ticket revenues for the four premier league men's professional team sports in the U.S. were $2.0 billion in 1996 (*Financial World* 1996).
8. The out-of-town tickets comprise 28 percent of combined total expenditures on sporting event tickets and would include tickets purchased to playoff tournaments and college football bowl games.
9. The difference in means is statistically significant at the 99 percent confidence level.
10. The topcoding threshold is now at $1 million annual income.
11. This approach was originally suggested to us by Allen Sanderson of the University of Chicago.
12. There are no football games in the sample because the data were collected during the spring and early summer of 1997.
13. Corporate marketing guides we obtained from the Baltimore Orioles (baseball) and Chicago Bears (football) reported income distributions of spectators that imply 1994 median incomes of $53,587 and $43,436, vis-a-vis the income estimates of $34,063 and $40,225, respectively, derived from the targets of game program advertising.   Thus, both teams are touting higher incomes for their customers than <u>any</u> of our estimates.
14. Among the four different sports, ice hockey ticket prices are the highest.

References

Baade, Robert A.   1987.   *Is There an Economic Rationale for Subsidizing Sports Stadiums?* Policy study no. 13, Heartland Institute, Chicago, Illinois.

———.   1994.   *Stadiums, Professional Sports, and Economic Development: Assessing the Reality.*   Policy study no. 62, Heartland Institute, Chicago, Illinois.

———.   1996.   "Professional Sports as Catalysts for Metropolitan Economic Development." *Journal of Urban Affairs* 18(1): 1–17.

Clotfelter, Charles T., and Phillip J. Cook.   1989.   *Selling Hope.*   Cambridge, Massachusetts: Harvard University Press.

Coats, Dennis, and Brad R. Humphreys.   1999.   "The Growth Effects of Sport Franchises, Stadia and Arenas."   *Journal of Policy Analysis and Management* 14(4): 601–624.

Financial World. 1996 (May 20). 165(8): 56–59.

Gorham, John, Peter Kafka, and Shailaja Neelakantan. 1998. "The Forbes 400: Bill Gates and Paul Allen Welcome 37 New Members to an Exclusive Club." *Forbes,* October 12: 165.

McElroy, Katherine Maddox, John J. Siegfried, and George H. Sweeney. 1982. "The Incidence of Price Changes in the U.S. Economy." *Review of Economics and Statistics* 64(2): 191–203.

Noll, Roger G., and Andrew Zimbalist. 1997. *Sports, Jobs, and Taxes.* Washington, D.C.: Brookings Institution.

Okun, Arthur M. 1975. *Equality and Efficiency: The Big Tradeoff.* Washington, D.C.: Brookings Institution.

O'Sullivan, Arthur. 1996. *Urban Economics.* Chicago: Irwin.

Pechman, Joseph A. 1985. *Who Paid the Taxes, 1966–1985?* Washington, D.C.: Brookings Institution.

Rosentraub, Mark S. 1997. *Major League Losers: The Real Cost of Sports and Who's Paying for It.* New York: Basic Books.

Siegfried, John J., Katherine Maddox McElroy, and George H. Sweeney. 1982. "Who Bears the Burden of Excise Taxes?" *Challenge* 25(2): 61–63.

Statistical Abstract of the United States. 1996. "Multimedia Audiences— Summary: 1996."

Zimmerman, Dennis. 1998. "Subsidizing Stadiums: Who Benefits, Who Pays?" In *Sports, Jobs and Taxes*, Roger G. Noll and Andrew Zimbalist, eds. Washington, D.C.: Brookings Institution, pp. 119–145.

4

Academics, Athletics, and Finances

Richard G. Sheehan
University of Notre Dame

In this paper I will present some statistics that attempt to relate collegiate athletics to finances and academics. I will not attempt to delineate the absolute relationship between athletic and financial success. My goal is more modest. I will be presenting instead some "data suggestions" that hopefully leave you with more questions than you came with.

Most of the data that I will present come from information released under the Equity in Athletics Disclosure Act (EADA), or the so-called Gender Equity reports. Every college that receives federal financial assistance in any form is now required to provide information relating to the distribution of a number of athletic variables by gender, including the number of athletes, the amount of financial aid, operating expenses, and implicitly, profits. These numbers are not without complexities. Each institution has its own accounting procedures, which typically are employed to facilitate internal decision making and not to ensure comparability with other academic institutions. Some of the reported numbers are therefore potentially misleading because of these accounting conventions. For example, one college might include telephone expenditures by the athletic department as a separate item charged to the department. Another might aggregate all telephone expenditures in a general account and may not explicitly charge the athletic department for its contribution to the overall bill. A few colleges require alumni to contribute a minimum amount like $100 to the university's general fund in order to be eligible to purchase football tickets. If 20,000 alumni make this contribution, $2 million per year is for the university's general fund that is really football-generated revenue. These examples should not lead you to conclude that the Gender Equity numbers cannot be trusted but rather to conclude that they must be interpreted with care.

Table 1 contrasts the Big Ten with the Mid-American Conference (MAC), of which Western Michigan is a member. The top part of the table presents a mix of statistics on enrollment, athletes, and some expenditures. The table is configured to present the conference averages, maximum, minimum, and the ratio of the minimum to the maximum. The final column presents the MAC average divided by the Big Ten average. The ratio of the minimum to the maximum within a conference yields one perspective on the degree of inequality within a conference, the ratio of the MAC to the Big Ten yields a perspective on the degree of inequality between the two conferences.

In terms of enrollment, the typical Big Ten institution is substantially larger than the typical MAC school; the only exception is Northwestern. The mix of male/female students is roughly similar for the two conferences. Big Ten schools typically have somewhat larger athletic programs. Despite the larger number of male athletes at Big Ten institutions, the Big Ten comes closer to meeting Title IX gender equity guidelines. (An institution can satisfy Title IX if its percentage of female student-athletes is roughly comparable with its overall percentage of females.) Of Big Ten scholarship athletes, 38.0 percent are female versus only 33.1 percent of MAC scholarship athletes. That puts the percentage of female scholarship athletes 11.2 percent below the percentage of female students at Big Ten schools versus 19.6 percent at MAC schools. This comparison is particularly important for an individual school because it is one way that a school can certify that it is in compliance with Title IX.

What causes this greater differential in MAC schools? Certainly alternative explanations are possible, and I would like to advance two. First, since Big Ten schools typically are larger, one could argue that they have access to more students to fill their athletic teams. Thus, reaching Title IX compliance may be easier for a larger school. A fundamental problem with this explanation, however, is that most scholarship athletes are recruited before they come to college, not from the student body. The second explanation focuses on the schools' individual capacities for generating funds to finance Title IX compliance. Table 1 indicates that the Big Ten generates substantial net revenue

Table 1 The Big Ten versus the Mid-American Conference

		Big Ten				MAC				MAC avg./
		Average	Maximum	Minimum	Min/max	Average	Maximum	Minimum	Min/max	Big 10 avg.
Enrollment:	Male	13,232	18,765	3,734	0.199	8,200	16,708	5,075	0.304	0.620
	Female	12.628	18,230	3,870	0.212	8,701	11,470	7,026	0.613	0.689
	% Female	49.2	54.4	43.3	0.796	52.8	58.1	34.2	0.589	1.072
Athletes:	Male	378	470	230	0.489	294	389	227	0.584	0.780
	Female	234	327	148	0.453	148	194	80	0.412	0.632
	% Female	38.0	41.3	30.2	0.729	33.1	40.6	25.8	0.636	0.871
	Diff.[a]	11.2	18.5	5.9	0.317	19.6	27.8	5.1	0.184	1.756
Student aid:	Male	$2,180,218	3,511,825	940,226	0.268	1,293,892	1,841,996	962,659	0.523	0.593
	Female	$1,335,507	2,536,923	506,501	0.200	646,408	823,056	443,458	0.539	0.484
	% Female	38.0	43.3	33.5	0.774	33.4	37.5	27.6	0.737	0.880
Op. exp:	BB[b]/men's	$480,473	1,301,433	209,106	0.161	134,848	274,546	66,404	0.242	0.281
	BB/women's	$250,460	510,255	107,587	0.211	77,130	122,165	58,074	0.475	0.308
	Football	$1,150,187	2,984,934	337,712	0.113	375,449	679,236	143,629	0.211	0.326
Total op. exp:	Men's	$2,345,423	5,068,365	971,449	0.192	716,258	1,164,957	369,786	0.317	0.305
	Men's sports excl. football	$1,195,239	2,083,431	633,737	0.304	340,809	485,721	226,157	0.466	0.406
	Women's	$922,097	1.843.743	474,199	0.257	276,978	476,055	162,984	0.342	0.300

(continued)

Table 1 (continued)

		Big Ten				MAC				
		Average	Maximum	Minimum	Min/max	Average	Maximum	Minimum	Min/ max	MAC avg./ Big 10 avg.
Recruit exp.	Men	$363,116	490,983	236,941	0.483	97,263	147,180	55,840	0.379	0.268
	Women	$127,797	176,004	70,505	0.401	32,272	64,995	20,858	0.321	0.253
Salaries	Men	$69,708	88,896	57,920	0.652	49,710	59,656	41,129	0.689	0.713
	Women	$47,032	57,467	39,946	0.695	36,231	45,281	28,550	0.631	0.770
Football	Revenue	$10,763,264	17,840,445	6,132,085	0.344	722,893	931,836	496,989	0.533	0.067
	Expense	$3,373,603	5,005,180	2,145,986	0.429	1,607,180	1,945,850	1,291,434	0.663	0.476
	Net	$7,389,661	15,512,024	2,665,632	0.172	(884,286)	(493,397)	(1,339,009)	2.714	-0.120
Men's BB	Revenue	$4,551,187	6,142,915	3,044,999	0.496	268,220	513,208	115,152	0.224	0.059
	Expense	$1,057,599	1,777,364	683,077	0.384	452,225	594,609	324,109	0.545	0.428
	Net	$3,493,589	5,459,838	2,226,199	0.408	(184,005)	(35,314)	(325,524)	9.218	-0.053
Men's other	Revenue	$569,884	2,658,212	15,202	0.006	100,668	364,455	—	0.000	0.177
	Expense	$2,244,463	3,329,909	1,568,489	0.471	884,143	1,411,663	537,871	0.381	0.394
	Net	($1,674,579)	246,513	(2,839,902)	(11.520)	(783,475)	(469,230)	(1,298,749)	2.768	0.468
Men	Revenue	$17,530,360	26,017,272	12,143,588	0.467	1,158,998	1,433,468	698,288	0.487	0.066
	Expense	$7,626,141	12,919,483	4,820,083	0.373	2,979,663	3,437,448	2,205,850	0.642	0.391
	Net	$9,904,220	19,655,268	3,540,421	0.180	(1,820,666)	(1,133,421)	(2,328,427)	2.054	-0.184

	average			min/max	average			min/max
Women								
Revenue	$779,356	3,064,266	24,697	0.008	37,915	78,808	780	0.010
Expense	$3,440,546	4,976,973	2,542,494	0.511	1,328,315	1,657,012	846,228	0.511
Net	($2,661,190)	(924,360)	(4,685,316)	5.069	(1,290,401)	(839,690)	(1,586,915)	1.890
Overall								
Revenue	$22,901,272	35,887,000	13,419,690	0.374	3,961,769	7,641,186	1,313,574	0.172
Expense	$19,448,095	36,302,000	7,391,879	0.204	5,781,812	7,455,973	4,466,822	0.599
Net	$3,413,177	18,730,905	(2,755,305)	(0.147)	(1,820,043)	185,213	(3,998,809)	−21.590
Revenue (%) Football	47.6	62.9	37.4		33.4	64.9	6.5	
Football + BB	69.7	99.4	53.0		52.6	99.9	12.1	
Cost (%) Football	17.3	13.8	29.0		27.8	26.1	28.9	
Football + BB	22.7	18.7	38.3		35.6	34.1	36.2	

The final column shows: 0.049, 0.386, 0.485, 0.173, 0.297, −0.533.

[a] The "average" columns show the difference between the percentage of females enrolled and the percentage of females who are athletes. The "min/max" columns show the ratio of the maximum and minimum values for this difference.

[b] BB = basketball

from its football and men's basketball programs and the MAC generates relatively little net revenue from these sports. Thus, the Big Ten
has a ready source of funds for subsidizing women's sports and complying with Title IX. One could argue that it is substantially easier for
the Big Ten to be able to afford to comply with the law. The data do
not prove that contention, but they certainly appear to suggest it.

Following the statistics on athletes in Table 1 are statistics on student aid, operating expenses for three sports (men's basketball,
women's basketball, and football), total operating expenses for men's
and women's sports, recruitment expenditures, and salaries. These
numbers suggest two basic conclusions.

Looking at the last column, the MAC average is consistently a
small fraction of the Big Ten average. The average coach's salary in
the MAC is about 75 percent of his or her Big Ten counterpart's.
Recruiting expenses are only 25 percent as high. Student aid is about
50 percent of the Big Ten average, and total operating expenditures are
roughly 30 percent of the Big Ten average. Thus, I have a very simple
question. Does anyone believe that across the board, year-in and year-
out, the MAC can compete with the Big Ten? The expenditure numbers suggest that the playing field is not level and that when MAC
schools play Big Ten schools, you should expect a mismatch. Now one
might be tempted to argue that the discrepancy in expenses is only in
Big Ten football. Unfortunately, that is far from the case. MAC
expenditures for female teams are also only 30 percent of those in the
Big Ten. You might alternately argue that higher Big Ten expenditures
reflect their greater number of athletes and, therefore, more teams.
That also is far from the case. On a per athlete basis, MAC expenditures are still less than 50 percent of Big Ten expenditures.

Why do we observe a discrepancy between Big Ten and MAC
expenditures? There are many hypotheses. Big Ten institutions may
have more legislative clout. They typically have more alumni. They
generally have longer athletic traditions. They may place greater
emphasis on intercollegiate athletics. Regardless of these hypotheses,
we will see in the bottom half of Table 1 that Big Ten schools definitely
generate more athletic revenue. I will leave it to you to postulate which
reasons are more important.

The second half of Table 1 presents revenues and expenses for various sports and categories, as well as for the overall athletic program.

Perhaps the most dramatic difference is in terms of football programs. The typical MAC football program is but a shadow of the typical Big Ten program. It is important to note, however, that athletic expenditures at the typical MAC institution are roughly 50 percent of those at a Big Ten school, but MAC revenues are less than 10 percent of the Big Ten average. Why the dramatic difference? Again, the numbers are suggestive but not definitive. One could argue that the marginal expenditures of the Big Ten so elevate their programs that they obtain the best athletes and coaches and can produce the best product, which is then marketed for millions of dollars in packed stadiums. Alternatively, one could argue that the tradition of the Big Ten has elevated the programs and generated their financial success. Or one could argue that the prior financial success of the Big Ten has bred a tradition that generates further financial and on-the-field success. In any event, the bottom line is that Big Ten football is a very lucrative endeavor on average, while MAC football is not.

Comparing averages in the Big Ten and the MAC, however, masks one other important difference in the conferences. There is much greater variation in the Big Ten than in the MAC in terms of football profitability. MAC losses range from $0.5 million to $1.4 million, a span of less than $1 million. In contrast, Big Ten profits range from $15.5 million to $2.7 million. There are a few teams that dominate Big Ten football profits: Michigan, Ohio State, and Penn State. On a year-in and year-out basis, these same teams are also at the top of the rankings, and one might readily argue that the correlation is not an accident. Three schools dominate Big Ten football profits and victories while no school dominates MAC football profits (or smallest financial losses) or victories. It appears then that rough financial parity has produced approximate on-the-field parity as well.

For men's basketball, the story is virtually identical to men's football. The only difference is the magnitude of the numbers. MAC expenditures run almost 50 percent of Big Ten expenditures, but revenues are less than 10 percent of the Big Ten's. The good news for MAC basketball is that, on average, MAC schools almost break even.

For other men's sports (so-called Olympic sports or nonrevenue sports), the situation changes dramatically. All schools in the Big Ten and the MAC lose money on these programs; the only difference is the magnitude of the losses. MAC schools spend only about 40 percent of

what Big Ten schools spend. The revenues in all cases are trivial compared with the size of the athletic budget. The good news for the MAC
is that it loses much less money in nonrevenue sports than the Big Ten.
The bad news for the MAC is that it loses less money because it spends
less, and one might reasonably project that spending less means winning less.

Given the substantial financial losses shown in Table 1 for other
men's sports, one might reasonably ask why schools spend so heavily
on these programs? One possible answer is that the National Collegiate Athletic Association (NCAA) requires a school to offer a minimum number of sports programs to field a Division IA football
program, but that minimum does not appear to be a binding constraint
on schools in the Big Ten or the MAC. Why, then, do they spend? If
they lose money and if they are not required to keep at least some of
these programs, why offer them? The acceptance of financial loss in
these programs suggests that the entertainment value placed on them is
higher. (One might argue that there is an educational value as well, but
that argument would be more appropriate for intramural activities than
for intercollegiate sports.)

Men's programs (all sports combined) generally are profitable in
the Big Ten but not in the MAC. The logic is simple. In the Big Ten,
football profits in particular make men's programs in general profitable. In the MAC, no football profits exist to offset other losses.

For women's sports, the story is similar to that for men's sports
other than football and men's basketball. Expenses are higher in the
Big Ten than in the MAC, and revenues for both are but a fraction of
expenses. (Women's revenues, however, are dramatically higher in the
Big Ten.) Once again, financial losses are lower in the MAC, but that
simply reflects the lower expenses. Returning to Title IX, Big Ten
schools fit the model frequently advanced that football "pays the bills"
and allows schools to offer a wide-ranging women's athletics program.
However, MAC schools dramatically contradict that model because
there are no football profits to offset other losses. In fact, the MAC
schools face even greater difficulties in complying with Title IX. That
is, total men's losses average $1.9 million, and total women's losses
are only $0.8 million. In the case of schools with roughly 50 percent
female students, an economist might argue that the financial subsidies
to men's and women's programs should be approximately equal to

meet the spirit of Title IX. The numbers in Table 1 suggest that could be done in alternative ways, for example, spending $1.1 million more on women's sports. However, all alternatives would impose potentially severe constraints on MAC schools because they lack financial resources.

The last four rows in Table 1 show the percentage of total revenues and expenses stemming from football and from football plus men's basketball, the two generally perceived "cash cows" of intercollegiate athletics. Institutional vagaries distort the maximums and minimums here, but the averages are revealing and suggest that football and men's basketball do generate the majority of revenues. However, although football programs in particular are perceived to be "gold-plated"—getting the most expensive versions of everything—the self-reported accounting numbers suggest that football does not comprise the majority of costs. The averages suggest that football and men's basketball do generate the majority of revenues, but they are not responsible for a majority of the expenditures.

Table 2 presents data from a more aggregate perspective. Rather than considering only the Big Ten and the MAC, Table 2 presents more limited summary information for all Division IA schools.[1] In general, the results are consistent with those in Table 1. Football and men's basketball are profitable, but other men's sports and women's sports

Table 2 Revenues and Expenditures at Division IA Schools

	Football	Men's basketball	Other men's sports	Women's sports
Division IA schools				
Revenue ($, millions)	6.27	2.40	0.24	0.59
Expense ($, millions)	3.26	1.02	1.28	2.42
Mean profit ($, millions)	3.01	1.38	−1.05	−1.83
Median profit ($, millions)	1.17	0.75	−0.98	−1.68
Division IA schools with a profit				
Reporting profit	71	75	3	4
Actual profit	38	61	0	0

SOURCE: Gender equity reports.

are not. The table reports both mean and median profits, because the distribution of football profits—and to a lesser extent the distributions of revenues and expenditures—is not a normal or bell-shaped distribution. A few schools make sizable profits like Michigan, Ohio State, and Penn State in the Big Ten. However, a small army of schools either barely break even or lose money, like all schools in the MAC. The mean profits of $3 million for football gives a misleading picture of the actual profit position of the typical Division IA institution, for which the median profit is only about $1.2 million.

Even that last number is misleading. The EADA reports from which these statistics are derived refer only to operating costs. Other costs such as debt service and administrative overhead can easily run in excess of $1 million. Thus, actual profits are likely much closer to zero than reported profits at the typical institution. For the Michigans and Ohio States, subtracting even $2 million in omitted costs only slightly changes the degree to which the football program is lucrative. For schools at the median, however, $1 million in increased costs dramatically changes reported profits.

The last rows in Table 2 indicate the number of programs reporting profits and the programs actually having profits after making adjustments for accounting peculiarities, debt service, and administrative overhead. The EADA reports suggest that about 75 percent of the 99 schools with complete reports make a profit in both football and men's basketball, and almost none make a profit in other men's programs or in women's programs. After adjusting the numbers to reflect all costs, however, the percentages with a profit drops to less than 50 percent in football, roughly 60 percent in men's basketball, and 0 percent in either other men's sports or in women's sports. The implication? Institutions that have large sports programs should receive substantial nonfinancial utility from those programs to make the expenditures worthwhile, or should at least believe that those programs and their publicity create additional student applications and a larger or higher-quality student body.

Table 2 presents a snapshot in time of the distribution of profits at Division IA football schools. How have profits changed over time? Focusing on football and men's basketball, the only programs with profits, the growth rate in average profits from 1983 to 1996 has been about 7.6 percent per year. This increase appears to be substantial and suggests that profits might improve dramatically even at institutions now currently suffering substantial losses. Unfortunately, that growth in profits has been highly uneven both over time and among institutions. In some years, profits at Division IA football schools have grown over 20 percent, and in other years they have actually decreased. In addition, profits at schools like Michigan have increased substantially while losses at MAC schools have shown no sign of abating.

Table 3 shows mean profits by conference as well as the 11 most profitable football and men's basketball programs. The numbers suggest that the best conferences do very well. The Southeastern Conference (SEC) and the Big Ten average profits of $8.6 million and $7.4 million, respectively, in football. In basketball, the Atlantic Coast Conference (ACC) joins them at the top. Again, it should be clear that some conferences—and by extension some schools—do very well, while others are engaged in a continuing financial struggle. Given the caveats mentioned already, it would appear that the Big Ten and the SEC as a whole are in strong shape. The ACC, Big East, Big 12, and Pacific–10 Conference (PAC) are generally surviving while the Western Athletic, USA, and Mid-American conferences are struggling to stay afloat. Again, I must note that some schools in almost every conference are doing well while others are not.

Table 4 presents profits of the 11 most profitable collegiate football and men's basketball programs. Arguably, the rankings are suspect because of institutional accounting inconsistencies. However, the results suggest certain points. First, some schools are very financially successful. The table includes representatives of the PAC (1), the SEC (5), the Big Ten (3), the Big 12 (1), and an independent. You might argue that Michigan or Notre Dame or Tennessee deserves to be ranked much higher, and I would not argue with you. Nevertheless, the point is that the most profitable football schools generate substantial revenue—even though their overall net revenues from football are relatively small. Second, looking at the list of most profitable football schools, one cannot avoid a comparison with the more traditional top 25 rankings; in particular, every school on the list is a regular in the top 25. Is that an accident? I sincerely doubt it. But the numbers—and the presumed correlation—cannot indicate causation. That is, does winning generate profits? Or does generating profits allow you to keep on winning? I will come back to this point shortly.

Table 3 Mean Profits by Conference[a]

Conference	Football ($, millions)	Men's basketball ($, millions)
Southeastern	8.60	2.60
Big Ten	7.39	3.49
Pacific–10	4.78	1.44
Big 12	3.46	1.26
Big East	3.09	0.81
Atlantic Coast	2.49	2.79
Western Atlantic	0.22	0.48
Conference USA	–0.70	1.19
Mid-American	–0.79	–0.20

[a] All calculations are based on all Division IA schools providing usable cost and revenue data in compliance with the Higher Education Act. All data are self-reported.

Table 4 The Eleven Most Profitable Programs[a]

	Football		Men's basketball	
Rank	School	Profits ($, millions)	School	Profits ($, millions)
1	Washington	20.3	Louisville	6.9
2	Florida	19.8	Arkansas	6.1
3	Auburn	16.8	Indiana	5.5
4	Penn State	15.5	North Carolina	5.4
5	Georgia	14.3	Arizona	5.3
6	Michigan	12.1	Kentucky	4.7
7	Alabama	12.1	Ohio State	4.6
8	Notre Dame	11.6	Iowa	4.1
9	Tennessee	11.3	Nebraska	4.1
10	Texas A&M	10.4	Florida State	3.8
11	Ohio State	10.2	Michigan	3.7

[a] All calculations are based on all Division IA schools providing usable cost and revenue data in compliance with the Higher Education Act. All data are self-reported.

The numbers in Table 4 also agree with those in Table 1 and show that football schools do not compete on a level field. In fact, no school from a "mid-major" or lower-rated conference appears on either top ten list. (One might argue that Louisville's ranking at the top of the men's basketball list is a contradiction. However, I would also argue that Louisville's ranking is likely boosted by institutional accounting since its EADA report indicates revenues almost $600,000 more than Kentucky's, a similar but potentially richer program, and costs less than 60 percent of Kentucky's.) Can a school other than a traditional power crack the top 10? The numbers suggest that it is dramatically easier for an institution like East Carolina or UNLV to break into the top echelon on the field than it is to break into the top tier in profits.

Let me next briefly address the question of causation. Does winning generate profits, for example? The evidence again must be viewed as suggestive rather than definitive. Statistical analysis (regression) of revenues does not indicate any strong relationship. In particular, it appears that winning more football games does not increase revenue but that a higher poll ranking does marginally improve profits. While that finding may appear contradictory, it should not be entirely unexpected. If Western Michigan and Michigan both win one additional game, will the win work to increase their revenues? The statistical answer is probably no. However, if Michigan is ranked slightly higher in the polls, will the elevated ranking increase its revenues? The statistical answer is likely yes. (One should also note that winning more would mean a higher ranking, so there could be a more indirect relationship between winning and revenues.) It might not be possible for Michigan to sell any additional tickets because they generally play before a full house. However, the school may become eligible for a better bowl or receive additional television revenue.

In terms of causation, what may be the most interesting result is that revenues appear to be largely driven by expenses. Based on the results shown in the previous tables, this interaction should come as no surprise. However, the question really should be about the magnitude of the increase in revenues. That is, if a school increases expenditures by $1, should it expect to increase revenues by more or less than $1? The answer to this question varies dramatically by sport. For other men's and women's sports, a $1 increase in expenditures increases revenues by $0.25 to $0.35 (Sheehan 2000). The implication? If a school wants to spend more money on these programs, it should feel free to do that, but it should not expect to earn its money back in increased revenues. For football, a $1 increase in expenditures generates approximately $1 in additional revenue (Sheehan 2000). The implication? If a school wants to keep throwing money at football, on average it will be no worse off with revenues increasing with expenditures. Thus, any incentive to follow this strategy must be based on a desire to win rather than a desire to make money.

The most interesting case is men's basketball, for which each $1 increase in expenditures is expected to produce approximately $2 in additional revenue (Sheehan 2000). This result may initially appear surprising, but I contend it is quite consistent with developments in Division I basketball. If schools generally observe that basketball expenditures are profitable, then they should invest in their basketball programs. The NCAA has myriad restrictions limiting institutions from simply dropping buckets of money into any sports program. However, the NCAA has few restrictions on schools adding basketball programs. The result? Almost 100 institutions have moved to Division I in basketball, arguably because they are investing in their basketball programs.

Finally, in terms of causation, one could ask whether schools use football revenues to subsidize other sports programs? (I focus on football rather than men's basketball because few schools generate enough net revenue from basketball to contribute appreciable subsidies to other sports programs.) The results suggest that higher net football revenue is associated with higher expenses in other men's and women's programs. For each $1 increase in football net revenue, regression results suggest that other men's expenditures rise by about $0.10 and women's expenditures rise by about $0.20 (Sheehan 2000). These numbers have two implications. First, although the values sound very small, top programs like Penn State share substantial additional revenues with women's sports. In fact, its football profits of $15.5 million give Penn State's women's sports about $3 million more to spend. Of course, there is also a downside. For a program like Tulane that lost $3.3 million on football, women's expenditures would be predicted to be down about $0.6 million. Second, if for each dollar of football net revenue, $0.10 goes to other men's sports and $0.20 goes to women's sports, where does the other $0.70 go? The answer, assuming no increase in

Table 5 Graduation Rates (1997)

Graduation rates	Big Ten average	Division IA average	10th percentile	90th percentile	MAC average	MAC avg./Big Ten	Athletes/all students[a]
All students	71.1	58.6	36.0	83.6	53.0	0.745	
Athletes	67.7	58.6	40.5	76.4	60.7	0.897	0.999
All students							
Black/M	45.4	39.3	18.0	65.8	32.2	0.710	
White/M	71.4	57.9	34.0	84.8	51.4	0.720	
Total/M	69.7	56.1	32.3	82.7	50.3	0.721	
Black/F	52.5	48.1	26.0	69.8	38.4	0.731	
White/F	74.5	63.0	41.2	88.0	56.4	0.757	
Total/F	72.6	61.1	38.6	84.7	55.1	0.759	
Athletes							
Black/M	49.4	43.2	23.0	67.8	43.0	0.871	1.099
White/M	66.5	57.7	40.2	75.0	59.7	0.897	0.997
Total/M	62.2	53.3	34.4	74.4	56.6	0.910	0.950
Black/F	66.8	62.5	33.0	92.0	60.3	0.902	1.300
White/F	82.0	70.1	52.4	88.0	69.6	0.849	1.112
Total/F	79.4	68.8	51.2	87.0	68.4	0.862	1.125
Football							
Black	51.8	43.9	20.0	66.0	46.5	0.897	1.118
White	71.0	61.9	46.0	79.0	63.7	0.897	1.070
Total	62.0	53.1	36.0	76.0	56.8	0.916	0.948

[a] Values calculated using data in "Division IA average" column.

administrative overhead, is that it would go back to the general fund of the institution. That is, colleges that have football profits are using those profits to subsidize the academic enterprise.

To this point I have said very little about academics, despite the title of this paper, which places academics first. Table 5 presents some statistics on graduation rates, which, although far from the only measure of academic performance, are the only readily available measure. Table 5 presents Big Ten and MAC average graduation rates as well as the average rates for all Division IA football schools and for the 10th and 90th percentiles. The table presents the graduation rates of the general student body and of athletes by sex and race. The last column shows that athletes—even football players—graduate at roughly the same rate as other students. In general, this is good news. (Basketball players, however, do not graduate at the same rate as the general student population.) Before any congratulations are handed out to football players and other athletes, however, a strong word of caution is in order. Athletes toil under substantial additional constraints because they must spend many hours in training or in sometimes intense competition. Critics of the current grant-in-aid system label their efforts "work" rather than athletics. Offsetting this cost, however, are some substantial benefits. In particular, athletes' grants-in-aid allow them to be full-time students without the distraction—at least until recently— of working to fund their tuition or board. In addition, they frequently have additional academic advantages, such as tutors who are not available to or are very expensive for a typical student. Thus, one might ask whether we should expect athletes to graduate at a higher rate than the student body in general.

Another frequently expressed concern is that major athletic programs place more emphasis on winning than studying and thus the most stress on student-athletes—or perhaps more accurately, on athlete-students. The results in Table 5, however, suggest that there is no support for this concern. If athletic competition were too stressful, we should expect to see lower graduation rates in the Big Ten than in the MAC. But, although the rates are close, Big Ten athletes have graduation rates that are slightly higher than those in the MAC. This result should not be surprising, however, given the results already presented. The Big Ten has dramatically more financial resources than the MAC.

To the extent that Big Ten schools value high graduation rates, they clearly have the ability to provide the resources to achieve that goal.

In summary, what should you conclude based on these statistics? I would argue that there are three general conclusions. First, athletic success and financial success are intimately related. Big-time schools with tradition and reputation may make money with their athletic programs; others do not. Furthermore, a "have-not" school has virtually no chance of changing (unless it cheats, but that is another story). Second, athletic programs generally cross-subsidize within their campuses. That is, the schools that make money can and do use those profits to improve nonrevenue sports as well as the institution's general academic program. However, the many schools with losses in their athletic programs are effectively using revenue generated from the academic arena to subsidize sports. There may well be a sound logic for this subsidy, but academics should insist that it be justified explicitly. Third, the academic enterprise is relatively insulated from the athletic enterprise except for what is often a relatively small financial link. Anecdotal evidence such as stories of the so-called "Flutie effect," in which applications double after a stunning athletic event, also link athletics to academics. However, the statistical evidence of any link is less than overwhelming. That should not imply that academics can safely ignore the athletic enterprise. It does, however, suggest that the athletic enterprise is likely to neither save nor destroy an institution.

Note

1. Table 2 excludes institutions not providing complete information: Boise State, Boston College, Houston, Michigan State, Pittsburgh, Rice, and Syracuse. In addition, it excludes the three service academies because they do not award athletic scholarships, and all students attending the academies receive full scholarship assistance.

References

Sheehan, Richard G. 2000. "The Professionalization of College Sports." In *Higher Education in Transition: The Challenges of the New Millennium*, Joseph Losco and Brian L. Fife, eds. Westport, Connecticut: Bergin and Garvey, pp. 133–158.

5

Economic Issues in the 1998–1999 NBA Lockout and the Problem of Competitive Balance in Professional Sports

Andrew Zimbalist
Smith College

The central problem of any professional team sports league is different from that of a typical industry. On the one hand, the National Basketball Association (NBA), the National Football League (NFL), the National Hockey League (NHL), Major League Baseball (MLB) and Major League Soccer (MLS) are each monopolies. On the other hand, unlike other monopolies, teams within each league compete on the playing field, but cooperate as businesses off the field.[1] Unlike General Motors and Chrysler, the Boston Red Sox would not benefit if competition drove the New York Yankees out of business. In fact, sports leagues need to cooperate in maintaining a certain level of competitive balance among their teams to preserve and enhance fan interest. That is, teams must be sufficiently equal in ability to ensure that the outcome of the games and season are in question.

The problem that professional sports leagues face in the 21st century is how to achieve this competitive balance when some teams represent cities that are eight times larger than the cities of their competitors, some teams play in state-of-the-art facilities and others do not, and some teams are owned by individuals or companies who potentially benefit from significant synergies between the team and their other businesses. While competitive balance is a longstanding problem in professional sports, it has taken on new dimensions since the advent of free agency in 1976, the introduction of the modern sports facility of the 1990s (which can increase team revenues by $20–$50 million or more a year), and the growing penetration of the ranks of team ownership by major media conglomerates.

Five strategies can be employed to address the problem of competitive balance:

1) Artificially restrict the growth of player salaries,

2) Introduce or increase revenue sharing among the teams with each league,

3) Further skew the reverse order draft of amateur players to favor low-revenue or low-rent clubs,[2]

4) Allow freer team movement among cities,[3] or

5) Compel league divestiture and engender competition.

The NBA lockout of 1998–1999 is an example of the first strategy, but the NBA already had a powerful mechanism to promote competitive balance in their league and the owners tried to eliminate it both in 1995 and in 1998. Thus, as I shall argue, contrary to the basketball owners' rhetoric about their concern for financially weak teams, their lockout was really just a bold attempt to boost profit margins.

BACKGROUND TO THE NBA LOCKOUT

In 1983, when free agency in professional sports was not yet a decade old, NBA Commissioner David Stern convinced NBA players' union director Larry Fleisher that NBA franchises were financially fragile and needed a salary cap to be economically viable. The cap was defined as 53 percent of defined gross revenues (DGR), which included only television, radio, and gate revenues. Both sides, however, agreed that the 53 percent should not be a hard cap and established certain exceptions that would allow teams to spend above the cap limit.

One such exception is called the "Larry Bird exception." This exception allows a team to re-sign one of its own players at any salary, regardless of whether the team has room under its salary cap to do so. For example, if the Chicago Bulls had spent $28 million on its first 11 players for 1998–1999 and Michael Jordan had changed his mind and decided to come back, even with the 1998–1999 team salary cap at $30 million the Bulls could have paid Jordan anything it wanted.[4] Without the exception, the Bulls could only pay Jordan the salary left under the cap, or $2 million.

Three characteristics of the Bird exception appealed to owners. First, giving teams an advantage in re-signing their own players meant that the roster would be more stable, and the owners believed that this stability would strengthen fan identification with the team. Second, together with the reverse-order draft (wherein teams at the bottom of the standings have earlier picks in the amateur draft each year), the Bird exception provided a hefty fillip to league competitive balance. Because the original signing team has a substantial advantage in re-signing its own free agents, superstar players signed out of college generally remain with their first team throughout their professional careers. In 1997–1998, 7 of the 11 top-paid players in the NBA still played for their original teams. Thus, if Michael Jordan had originally signed with Milwaukee or Utah instead of Chicago, he probably would have played in those cities throughout his career. The Bird exception, then, is a powerful force preventing the rich teams from accumulating all the best players.

This observation is reinforced by the weak statistical correlation between team salaries and team win percentage in the NBA since the introduction of the salary cap. Using annual data for 1984–1985 through 1997–1998, the coefficient of determination between these two variables is between 0.30 and 0.40 in only 2 of the 14 years, between 0.20 and 0.30 in 5 of the years, between 0.10 and 0.20 in 5 other years, and below 0.10 in 2 of the years.[5]

Third, the Bird exception with the salary cap still provides a break on superstar salaries relative to a more open system of free agency. This is because most teams will not have enough room under their cap to bid effectively for a superstar. The star player, then, generally will not receive competitive bids for his services and will not necessarily end up where his marginal revenue product is the highest. If the Bird exception was the price the owners had to pay to get the union to agree to a cap system, then it was a price well worth paying.

Both sides agreed that the Bird exception was an ingenious and productive institution for the NBA until the 1995 negotiations, when the owners called for its elimination. In 1995, with average player salaries at $1.44 million and with Simon Gourdine installed as the players' union (NBPA) director, the owners saw an opportunity to slow down salary growth. Gourdine, oddly enough, had worked as an executive in the NBA's central office between 1970 and 1981, the last seven of those years as deputy commissioner. Gourdine acceded to major concessions proposed by Commissioner Stern, only to provoke a player movement to decertify the union. Eventually, the players accepted a deal that gave the owners a three-year rookie salary scale, as well as new restrictions on free agents, and eliminated a middle-range salary exception. The Bird exception was preserved, albeit somewhat weakened. The decertification drive had badly divided the players, the agents, and the union. When it was all over, the player representatives to the union voted to oust Gourdine in February 1996. Several months later he was replaced by Billy Hunter.

In spite of these changes, league revenues and player salaries grew handsomely in the ensuing three years. With payrolls growing faster, the salary share of basketball-related income (BRI)[6] rose from 53 percent in 1995–1996, to 55 percent in 1996–1997, to 57 percent in 1997–1998.[7] This growth, of course, was acceptable to the players, but they were concerned that, with the elimination of a middle-salary exception[8] in the 1995 agreement, salaries were becoming too stratified. Despite the growth in the average salary to $2.4 million in 1997–1998,[9] between 1995–1996 and 1997–1998, the number of players earning the minimum salary almost doubled to 60 and the number earning less than $1 million grew to 151.

The owners' concerns were different. Individual salaries were hitting unprecedented peaks, and some young stars who had scarcely demonstrated their potential value were receiving long-term, mega-salary contracts. As a consequence, the players' salary share was increasing and the owners saw no end to this growth. Further, the owners knew that a) the union still had some scars from its bitter internal battles in 1995; b) the union had a new director who had no direct experience in collective bargaining; c) growing salary stratification could further undermine union solidarity; and d) strong, ongoing revenue growth allowed the owners to offer the players absolute salary growth even with a decreasing share of the total pie. The owners again saw an opportunity to restrain salary growth and they seized it. On July 1,

1998, the owners imposed a lockout. One of the owners' demands was that the Bird exception be eliminated.

ECONOMIC ISSUES IN THE LOCKOUT

The owners claimed that the league had become unprofitable and that more than half the teams lost money in 1997–1998. However, the players were never given detailed team financial statements for 1997–1998 to allow them to confirm this extravagant claim. But they did receive this information for 1996–1997 and previous years. The union hired Stanford economist Roger Noll to decode the books. Based on Noll's work, the union concluded that no more than four or five teams out of 29 actually lost money in 1996–1997.

To understand the union's suspicion about ownership accounting practices, it is instructive to review some collective bargaining history in the NBA. Following the 1988 collective bargaining agreement (CBA), which defined DGR as revenues derived from, related to or arising out of the performance of players in NBA basketball "games," a dispute arose over what sources of income should be included.[10] Owners divided luxury suite revenue into two parts: the rental payment for the comfort and convenience of the suite and the ticket price for watching the game. The owners claimed that the latter belonged to DGR and the former did not. This and similar issues led the players to bring an arbitration complaint against the owners, which they eventually won in 1992 for a settlement of some $60 million.

When the 1995 CBA was signed, DGR was changed to BRI and the players accepted a lower share (48.04 percent) in return for a broader definition of revenues applicable to the cap. The 1995 BRI included all basketball income except naming rights, 60 percent of signage and luxury box revenues, certain property income, and part of related-party income.

The 1995 CBA took 11 pages to define BRI, and it was still subject to regular disputation. Suppose you are an owner negotiating an arena lease and are given a choice: pay $2 million in rent and receive 50 percent of a projected $4 million in signage income or pay no rent and receive no signage. It might seem that this is a choice between equals, but since the CBA gives 40 percent of signage income to the players, the owner would do better with the second option of no rent/no signage. Lease agreements offer manifold opportunities for such juggling, especially when the arena and team are owned by the same person or entity.

Related-party transactions are a central component of the finances for most teams. If the owner of the team also owns the arena, the arena management company, the concessionaire rights, a local TV or radio station, Web pages, local real estate, law, or consulting firms that do business with the team, then the owner has tremendous latitude about where to make his or her profits appear. Abe Pollin, for example, owns the new MCI Center in Washington, D.C., where both his NBA and NHL teams, the Washington Wizards and Capitals, play. He can retain arena revenue from naming rights, premium seats, signage, catering, and theme activities in his arena corporation, thereby reducing the revenues earned by his teams by tens of millions of dollars annually. Almost half of all NBA team owners also own their facilities while several others own companies that have management contracts for their arenas.

Owners can also pay themselves exorbitant salaries and consulting fees as well as receive extensive perquisites. They can choose to capitalize their franchises through owner loans rather than paid-in capital and take their returns in the form of interest income (which shows up as costs on the team ledgers) rather than profits. Thus, Wayne Huizenga, owner of the Marlins (until February 1999), Dolphins, Panthers, Pro Player Stadium, Sports Channel Florida, and arena management and concessionaire ventures, could rechannel his teams' revenues to his other related businesses, making the 1997 world champion Marlins appear to lose money.[11]

In leagues where there is a salary cap, such accounting legerdemain comes in handy to reduce player payrolls. Where there is no cap, owners have still preferred to hide profits to reduce revenue-sharing payments or to argue for larger public stadium subsidies, collective bargaining concessions or special treatment under the law.

So, when the NBPA reviewed the teams' pre-1997 financial records, it could not discover a basis for the owners' claims of declining profits. The few teams that lost money in 1996–1997 generally did not have losses in prior years. Moreover, each of these teams would have a new arena to play in within two years. New arenas usually raise a team's revenues by $20–$30 million a year. Moreover, the NBA had signed a new four-year television contract with NBC and Turner that would begin with the 1998–1999 season and increase the average annual payout per team from a guaranteed $9.5 million to a guaranteed $22.8 million. Thus, even if four or five teams had true financial difficulties in 1996–1997, it seemed that new arenas and television money would wash away their problems.

The NBPA also wondered why the owners were so alarmed that player salaries had increased to 57 percent of BRI. By comparison, the NFL was using a different, narrower revenue concept and setting its salary cap at 63 percent of defined revenues. But the NFL cap also had loopholes, albeit fewer than the NBA's, and its salaries frequently rose to 70 percent of defined revenues. If the NFL's defined revenue concept were converted to the NBA's BRI, the salary share in the NFL would have hovered around 60 percent in recent years. In Major League Baseball (MLB), the comparable player share was also around 60 percent, excluding the additional 12 percent that the teams spend on their player development systems. (For the NBA, the latter is an expense that is borne almost entirely by college basketball programs.)[12] Furthermore, an NBA team played half the number of games as an MLB team, had half the number of players for whom it has to pay for travel, lodging and meals, has fewer coaches, smaller facilities and less equipment. Therefore, could not NBA teams still be profitable with player shares around 60 percent?

Other facts as well undermine the owners' claim to dwindling profits. The NBA lavishes alluring sums on its coaches and front office personnel. In 1997–1998, Commissioner David Stern reportedly earned $8 million a year, far in excess of his counterparts in the other sports. The salaries of head coaches and general managers more than tripled between 1994–1995 and 1997–1998. Fourteen head coaches received over $2.8 million a year, with one coach's salary reaching up to $8 million. In contrast, the three highest paid coaches in the NFL each earned under $2.5 million a year, although each had won a Super Bowl. Asked to comment about the astronomical increases in NBA coaches' salaries, David Stern commented to the Web site Sportsline USA: "If the owners spend all that money on coaches, that means they have it. Otherwise, they wouldn't do it."

Consider what would happen to NBA profitability if the players salary share remained at 57 percent. In its December 14, 1998 issue (p. 130), *Forbes* magazine estimated that the average NBA team earned $6.6 million in profits during 1997–1998.[13] To be conservative, let us take half of this figure and round down and, thus, assume that the average profits were only $3 million. The average team, then, would have financial results that looked something like this in 1997–1998:

Team revenues = $60 million
Player salaries = $34 million
Other costs = $23 million
Profit = $3 million

Now assume, as the NBA did in its projections, that revenues grow at 12 percent annually. For player salaries to retain their 57 percent share, they would also have to grow at 12 percent.

The owners had long argued to the players that they needed artificial constraints on salary growth because they were unable to behave rationally given the pressure they are under from the fans and the media to sign the best players. That is, they need protection from themselves when it comes to player salaries. Granting the owners this dubious premise, it certainly cannot also apply to their other expenses. Costs like plane travel, hotels, arena maintenance, front office personnel, and coaching staff should more or less follow the underlying rate of inflation. Let us generously assume that the "other costs" category will grow at 5 percent annually, approximately two times the current rate of inflation. Now, consider what would happen to profits under this scenario. As the share of player salaries stays the same, the share of other costs falls rapidly and, hence, the share of profits rises. As the share of profits in revenue grows, and revenues grow at 12 percent, absolute profits exhibit explosive growth. By the year 2002–2003, the average team would have these results:

Team revenues = $105.8 million
Player salaries = $59.9 million
Other costs = $29.3 million
Profits = $16.6 million

That is, profits would grow more than fivefold over the period; the annual growth rate of profits would be 40.8 percent!

Would $16.6 million represent a fair return for a team owner? On revenues of $105.8, this is a 15.7 percent return. This is approximately three times the average, pretax rate of return on revenues in the leisure-time industry in the United States between 1990 and 1997 of 5.8 percent.[14]   Even if we assumed that in 1997–1998 the average NBA team earned zero profits (instead of $3 million) and other costs were $26 million (instead of $23 million), at the assumed rates of growth, average team profits in 2002–2003 would be $12.6 million, or 11.9 percent of revenues.

It is, of course, theoretically possible that even with such strong average profits, the distribution of profits might be so unequal as to leave a handful of teams in financial difficulty. However, with the new arenas projected for the bottom teams and the nearly two-and-a-half fold increase in the national television contract, which is divided equally among all teams, it is likely that even the financial bottom dwellers would have acceptable rates of return.

If some teams had true financial problems, then the players' association believed that they should have been addressed through additional revenue sharing among the owners rather than through new artificial restraints on salaries.   Unlike the NFL or MLB, the NBA does not share any local revenues. The NFL teams share net gate revenue 60/40 percent between the home and visiting team.[15] They also share permanent seat license and club seat revenue under certain circumstances. Baseball introduced a new revenue sharing system in 1996 wherein the top revenue team would be transferring approximately $18 million to the bottom team in 1999. Finally, it is important to recall that a significant part of the return from owning a sports team may not show up in the profit and loss statement. Apart from their ability to manipulate related-party transactions, owners reap substantial tax sheltering benefits from player amortization schemes. They also benefit from capital gains, psychic income, ability to aid their other businesses, political access, and perquisites.

It is the total economic return that buyers consider when they contemplate owning a sports team. The definitive measure of this total economic return is the franchise value, which is determined in the marketplace. The value only rises when the economic return to ownership rises. And here the numbers speak loudly and clearly: expansion fees for an NBA franchise were $32.5 million in 1988 and $125 million in 1994. In November 1998, the New Jersey Nets sold for $150 million. The Nets were ranked by Forbes as the fourteenth most valuable NBA team out of twenty-nine in 1998, or, basically, in the middle of the pack.[16] Based on these figures, NBA franchises have increased in value nearly fivefold over the last ten years. This would not have happened if there were not a substantial and growing economic return to ownership.

ASSESSING THE NEW COLLECTIVE BARGAINING AGREEMENT

Some sportswriters, player agents, and even the guru of sports union leaders, Marvin Miller, have questioned the efficacy of union leadership during the recent NBA lockout. While the final 1998–1999 CBA makes some significant concessions from the players' perspective, the deal also contains some important gains for the union. Moreover, both the structure of the deal and the union's accrued experience from the process augur well for the next confrontation in 2005–2006. The critics are right when they argue that Billy Hunter and Patrick Ewing, the union president, may have made some mistakes. They are wrong if they believe that Hunter and Ewing did not do a superlative job under the circumstances.

The two significant concessions made by the union were accepting a near hard cap at 55 percent of defined revenues during years four through six of the agreement[17] and accepting a limit on individual player salaries. Marvin Miller critiqued the deal, asserting that the role of unions is to set minimum not maximum wages. Fair enough, but Miller leaves out the following facts: a) the NBA has had a salary cap, albeit porous, since 1983; b) the union was coming off a near devastating bargaining process in 1995 which sharply divided the players and resulted in greater salary stratification; c) the NBA players had no prior experience with work stoppages; d) the economic conditions of the 1990s are far different than those that prevailed in baseball when

Miller's players' union cut its teeth; and e) the NBA owners conducted a very controlled, deliberate, and sophisticated lockout.

Under the new deal, the salary cap remains at 48.04 percent of defined revenues, and it remains subject to various exceptions. These exceptions will allow team payrolls to go up to 55 percent of defined revenues without any additional restraint. If aggregate payrolls go above this percentage, however, the players will reimburse the owners dollar for dollar of any overage up to 60.5 percent of revenues. If payrolls go above this latter level, then the owners whose teams' payrolls exceed the 60.5 percent threshold will pay a 100 percent tax on every dollar of salary above this level. Thus, there are strong constraints built into the system to keep player compensation expenses at 55 percent of defined revenues in net terms, but there is certainly some wiggle room. The point here is that the current deal has evolved out of the existing salary cap institution. It was not created out of thin air.

What is new, even to basketball, is the acceptance of an absolute limit on individual salaries. For 1999, the limits are $9 million for players with less than 7 years of service, $11 million for players with between 7 and 9 years, and $14 million for players with 10 or more years. These limits will rise in step with NBA revenues and no existing player will be forced to take a cut thanks to a grandfathering provision that allows any salary to grow by 5 percent over its previous level. Further, these limits apply to the first year of a contract, but contracts for Bird free agents can extend for seven years and grow at 12 percent of the base salary per year. If these limits had been in place during the last CBA, only three players would have been affected directly. The potential problem here is not whether Patrick Ewing makes $20 million or $14 million (Ewing forfeited $8 million of his 1998–1999 salary from the lockout), it is that historically the star players were the salary trailblazers for the entire league.

The owners stand to reap some handsome profits from these limitations. If net salaries remain at 55 percent of defined revenue,[18] then under the assumptions in the new profit model, an average owner's profits would grow to $18.7 million in 2002–2003 on revenues of $105.8 million. Because of the wiggle room in the system, however, it is likely that some owners will go through the 60.5 percent trigger and raise the overall net player share somewhat above 55 percent.

One problem that basketball has had for many years and that was exacerbated by the 1995 CBA is that the cap system, without sufficient exceptions for mid-range players, generated a sharp class system among the players. Rather than pulling up all salaries, the superstars were forcing the salaries of most other players downward by occupying increasing amounts of cap room. This created not only a problem of equity but also a problem for union solidarity that did not go unnoticed by the owners.

The new CBA scores appreciable gains for the players in recreating a middle-range salary scale. For instance, a new "middle class" exception was added at $1.75 million for 1999, rising to the league average salary in 2003. Teams can sign one player per year to one six-year contract under this exception, even if the team has reached its 48 percent cap. Thus, by year six of the deal, some teams may have 6 of its 12 players paid the league average salary. The union also scored significant gains in minimum salaries, which now range from $287,500 to $1 million, depending on years of service, and substantial improvements in player retirement benefits.

Price regulation always creates strange outcomes. In the case of the NBA cap, we are already seeing that some excellent (but not superstar quality) players have had their salaries shoot up to the maximum. That is, instead of having, say, a Patrick Ewing at $18 million and a Latrell Sprewell at $10 million, we might find them both at $14 million. And other players whose salaries are effectively constrained by the maximum may find that the owners will give them a seven-year deal at the maximum, instead of what, absent the new limits, might have been a five-year deal at a few million more per year. This possibility will be especially beneficial to older veterans. In other words, the owners will find a way to pay the players.

It is apparent that in the short run, a majority of players will either gain from or be unaffected by this new CBA. The 55 percent threshold is essentially the 57 percent the players attained in 1998 without Michael Jordan's salary. This is the key to understanding the union's dilemma and the eventual outcome.

In the early and mid 1970s, when Marvin Miller fashioned the impressive solidarity and militance among baseball players, the minimum salary in baseball was $16,000 (in 1975) and the average salary was $44,676 (in 1975). An average baseball player who sat out a whole season in 1975 would then lose less than one-fiftieth of what an average NBA player in 1998–1999 would lose. Moreover, the potential gains in 1975 for the baseball players were astronomical if they could move from the reserve system to a system of free agency.

Union director Billy Hunter did not have these advantages in 1998. Nor did he have the advantage of a union with any history of struggle and sacrifice. In their book *Money Players,* Armen Keteyian, Harvey Araton, and Martin Dardis said this about the state of union politics in 1994: [Charlie] Grantham (then union director) knew his players were not about to strike or tolerate being locked out. Worse still, Hunter inherited a union that was bitterly divided over a failed decertification vote in 1995 and highly unequal salary distributions.

The absence of a history of collective bargaining struggle is not just the absence of an abstract notion of solidarity. Collective bargaining involves establishing practices of cohesion and strategic communication. Hunter faced strong criticism for being both too authoritarian and too democratic. On the owners' side, democracy was not an issue. Commissioner David Stern called the shots and spoke for the 29 owners. Hunter needed to lead, but he could not get too far out in front of his 400 players.

In October 1998, Hunter called a meeting for all union members in Las Vegas. The issues and positions were exhaustively debated in small and large groups. The meetings were open only to players and union staff, but it was clear within days that David Stern knew what was discussed and decided upon in Las Vegas. Indeed, individuals from the Commissioner's office have suggested that they had informants all along and knew about every move the union made.

Hunter was also accused of being David Falk's puppet and, sometimes, Arn Tellum's. Large parts of the media uncritically regurgitated these claims. Yet anyone involved in the process, who spent time in the union office or knew the deep integrity of Billy Hunter, knew that these charges were utter nonsense. To be sure, the willingness of the union staff initially to discuss and then accept limits on high-end salaries ran diametrically counter to the interests of the big-time agents.

On the other hand, Hunter developed a wonderful rapport with the players and his staff. He fashioned a strong unity out of division, and he held the players together for several months of the lockout—itself a Herculean feat. While the final settlement terms were not everything the union wanted, they were a very long way from the owners' original demands and even from the owners' position when they supposedly made their last offer in late December. What is remarkable about both the process and the outcome is that under the circumstances Billy Hunter and the union accomplished as much as they did.

In the future, the union will have this negotiating experience under its belt and player salaries will be more compressed because of the mid-range exemptions. Both changes augur well for union solidarity and strength. Most important, the vast majority of NBA players are pleased with the present deal and, therefore, with their union experience.

The first salary results from the new CBA are already in, and so far it looks good for the players. They have increased their share in defined revenues to approximately 59 percent (on a nonprorated basis), even without Michael Jordan's salary, which took up about 2 percentage points. The average player salary jumped to $2.8 million in 1998–1999. Moreover, the players clearly have resurrected the middle-salary range. On a nonprorated basis, the median player salary rose by more than 20 percent from $1.4 million to $1.7 million. In 1998–1999, 13 players signed for the mid-level exception and 20 veteran players signed for the new veteran minimum salary of $1 million. All told, in 1998–1999 there were 120 players with salaries between $1 million and $2 million, compared with only 74 in the category in 1997–1998. Further, the number of players with salaries below $1 million fell from 151 in 1997–1998 to 101 in 1999, and the number below $500,000 fell from 85 in 1997–1998 to 40 in 1999.[19] Of course, the more problematic years four through six of the new CBA (when the escrow tax kicks in for player shares above 55 percent) are yet to come, but most players cared more about the first three years and getting back to work.[20]

THE NBA DEAL AND THE Y2K PROBLEM

Not surprisingly, the NBA's new salary constraints and strong profit expectations caught the attention of baseball and hockey owners. For instance, Carl Pohlad, owner of the Minnesota Twins, praised the salary control aspects of the NBA deal and asserted: "We've got to have some deal like the NBA's if we are to survive."[21]

Can we expect to find NBA-type changes in 2002 and 2003 when the new MLB and NHL deals are negotiated? More generally, how does the NBA deal fit into the changing landscape of professional sports?

It is by now a cliche to note that the ownership of professional team sports is changing. By one estimate, in early 1998, 66 public corporations had direct or indirect ownership interests in sports teams: 31 in MLB, 30 in the NHL, and 20 in the NBA. A large share of these public companies are in the media business. Media-business-owned teams often have a different objective than other teams; namely, the team itself is not necessarily viewed as a profit center, but rather as "software" or programming to promote the larger media empire. For example, when FOX decided to pay the 33-year-old Kevin Brown $105 million over seven years beginning with the 1999 season, part of the expected payoff was that Brown's stature would help promote the FOX network in the United States and abroad. CBS' gargantuan contract with the NFL is buying football along with its ratings as well as exposure and status for its other programming. In the fall of 1998, CBS led the networks in prime time ratings. It is the first time CBS has topped the charts this deep in the season since 1993, which was the last time CBS had the NFL.[22]

Fifteen million dollars a year for a 40-year-old pitcher seven years into the future is a lot of money and probably would not make sense viewed from the perspective of a single baseball team. However, Rupert Murdoch thinks Brown is worth at least $105 million to his News Corporation, and he likely is right; but it is questionable whether Brown would have been worth this much to the Los Angeles Dodgers baseball team alone.

In early 1998, the 30 owners of MLB teams were debating whether to allow Murdoch and his News Corporation to buy the Dodgers. After their reported unanimous vote to allow the purchase, I asked one owner if the baseball community didn't have some serious reservations about this sale. His reply was, "We didn't have a choice." He was referring to the fact that the FOX regional sports network already had local contracts to televise 24 of baseball's 30 teams. But there was another element as well. FOX was about to offer $310 million for the Dodgers, by far the highest purchase price for a team in baseball's history.   Baseball's owners were happy to have Murdoch push up the value of their teams, but now when Murdoch also breaks the salary scale, the owners cry that he is upsetting competitive balance.

The media-company-as-team-owner phenomenon is just the latest irritant to the competitive balance mixture in professional team sports. Owners have long argued that teams from larger cities had an advantage over those from smaller cities; and, especially in the 1990s, teams with new facilities generating tens of millions of dollars in additional revenues were seen as having a competitive edge over teams playing in older facilities. That is, a team from a large city or with a new facility or owned by a media conglomerate would be able and willing to outbid other teams to procure top player talent.

In theory, this argument always made some economic sense. In practice, however, the advantaged teams were not dominating their leagues (save in baseball during the pre–free agency, predraft era). Indeed, some even argued that it would have been in the leagues' best financial interests if the big city teams did dominate because having those teams in the playoffs would raise aggregate fan interest along with television ratings.

Beginning in the mid 1990s, however, the big-city/new-facility/ media-owned teams in baseball began to monopolize the postseason landscape. During the 1998–1999 offseason, many of the other teams publicly gave up and waived a white handkerchief before the season began. Owners such as Carl Pohlad, whose net worth is $1.3 billion according to *Forbes*, decided that maintaining a payroll in the $25–$45 million range would not allow them to win their divisions. Therefore, their profit-maximizing strategy is to minimize their payrolls to $10–$15 million. Pohlad now follows the ignominious example of his fellow owner Wayne Huizenga. Each attempted to punish his fans for not supporting the team in the building of a new stadium with public funds.[23]

While the revenue disparity between the richest and poorest baseball team was around $30 million in 1989, by 1998 it was close to $120 million. To this volatility, add the presence of new franchise owners who also own international communications networks and who value their ballplayers not only by what they do on the field but what they do for their networks. Further, baseball's expansion by four teams in the

1990s, while adding excitement to the game, diluted the talent pool and made the star players stand out more and, thereby, made it easier to buy a winning team.

Baseball tried to address these inequalities in the last collective bargaining agreement. However, it is now clear that the agreement's plan to share revenue among the teams (wherein in 1999 the top team with revenues around $200 million would transfer approximately $18 million to the bottom team with revenues around $40 million) and the luxury payroll tax (wherein the top five payroll teams in 1999 would pay a 34 percent tax on that portion of team salaries above approximately $76 million) did not go nearly far enough toward leveling the imbalances.

Consider these statistics. In 1998, of the 8 teams that made the playoffs, all were among the top 12 teams in payroll. Further, of these top 12 teams, all had winning percentages above 0.500, save the Baltimore Orioles who finished at 0.488. Of the bottom 18 teams in payroll, only 2 teams finished above 0.500. Of the bottom ten teams in payroll, none finished above 0.475. Put differently, in 1998 no team made the playoffs without spending at least $47 million on payroll, and no team spending less than $38 million had a winning record.

Some of these results, no doubt, are from poor management or owner machinations. But others have to do with the underlying institutions and incentives of ownership in Major League Baseball.

With varying degrees of success, the NFL, the NHL, and the NBA have avoided the pitfall of advantaged-team domination. The NFL formula is simple: extensive revenue sharing among the owners, reverse order draft, unbalanced schedule, prohibition against corporate ownership, and a fungible salary cap set at 63 percent of league-defined gross revenues. The NHL formula entails curtailing unrestricted free agency until a player reaches 31 years of age, limitations on player sales, and a reverse order draft. The NBA, as we have seen, albeit dominated in recent years by the big-city Chicago Bulls, owes the strength of many of its small-city teams, such as the Utah Jazz, to the Larry Bird exception to its salary cap.

If and when competitive balance problems manifest themselves in other sports, as they appear to be doing now in baseball, affected leagues would do well to study the NFL example of revenue sharing. By dividing equally all revenue from the national television contract (an average of $2.2 billion a year over the next eight years) and national licensing, splitting the net gate 60/40, as well as sharing other revenue sources, the NFL has attained unprecedented balance. Though arguably the NFL's system should be modified because the league offers owners little or no profit incentive to win.

The NBA response to revenue inequality among its teams has been to attempt to lower the player share in league revenue and to turn the soft cap into a hard cap. That is, the NBA has made the players bear the burden of revenue inequality among the owners. Baseball owners attempted a similar solution in 1994–1995. In both cases the outcome was predictable—a lengthy work stoppage. At the very least, the burden of dealing with inequalities needs to be shared. Players should accept some additional restraints, but owners need to do additional revenue sharing. Further, to guard against free riding, teams should be required to meet certain payroll standards (e.g., 80 percent of average league payroll) to qualify as a beneficiary of revenue sharing.

In January 1999, MLB Commissioner Bud Selig, seemingly inspired by the new NBA and the lofty contract for Kevin Brown, formed a committee to study the issue of competitive balance in baseball. Selig appointed several luminaries to the committee, including former Federal Reserve head Paul Volcker and former U.S. Senator George Mitchell, along with several owners. Although some technical questions exist within the issue of competitive balance, the more important and less tractable problems are political. Without union representatives, Selig's committee risks generating solutions that appeal to only one side.

In 1994, the baseball owners, after studying competitive balance, convinced themselves that a salary cap was needed, but they never convinced the players. The result was a strike and no World Series that year. Even if baseball owners eventually decide that the solution is more revenue sharing among themselves rather than new artificial constraints on salaries, the nature of the sharing is something that the union must ratify.

Of course, it is far from simple to convince advantaged owners to increase revenue sharing by voluntarily taxing themselves. These owners would argue that they paid more for their advantaged franchise and that additional taxation amounts to a form of asset confiscation. However, unbalanced competition and work stoppages will also lower the value of their asset—and possibly by more than additional revenue sharing.

It is a stretch to think that the new NBA deal is easily transferable to baseball or hockey, which have never operated with a salary cap. Indeed, both the NFL and NBA caps were around in 1994–1995 during the last negotiations in hockey and baseball.[24] The MLB and NHL owners were emboldened, but so were the players.

If owners and players are unable to resolve the problem of competitive balance on their own, then it will be up to Washington politicians to awaken from their long-standing sports slumber. The natural economic solution for professional sports is competition. With two leagues in each sport, monopoly teams in big cities will soon find another team from the competing league in their territory. The artificial shortage of teams will evaporate and deserving cities will no longer have to compete against each other through public subsidies to get teams. This will erode the competitive imbalance problems from new facilities and larger cities.

The public policy solution is straightforward: pass legislation that will break each league up into competing business entities.

Notes

1. In reality, teams in these leagues both cooperate and compete as businesses, but it is their cooperation in certain areas that distinguishes them from other businesses.
2. For instance, in a league with 30 teams, the first 15 picks could be given to the bottom 15 clubs in reverse order to finish in the previous season. The next 15 picks could go to the 15 clubs with the lowest revenue or rent (potential revenue from site). The third 15 picks could go to the top 15 clubs in reverse order of their finish, etc. "Rent" refers to potential revenue given the characteristics of the city and site. Internationalizing the draft along with our rule changes would also benefit competitive balance.
3. Although this strategy has been employed in all leagues (though not in baseball since 1972), the NFL experience shows it can be problematic. In particular, it can create political problems in the abandoned city and eventually force the league to add an expansion team in order to restore a team to the city. Should this occur, the league loses some control over its output and, hence, some of its monopoly power.
4. Actually, under the new agreement Jordan's salary could not increase by more than 5 percent. Because his salary last year was $33 million, the Bulls could have paid Jordan $34.65 million in 1998–1999 (prorated for the number of games played in the shortened season).

5. The correlation is even weaker when team salary was lagged a year and when MSA population was controlled. Quirk and Fort (1999) present rank correlation statistics that show this relationship is stronger in the NBA than the other leagues in the 1990s. It is likely that this tighter correlation in the NBA can be explained entirely by the Bulls' exceptional success and high payroll due to the presence of Michael Jordan.

6. See definition in text, p. 97.

7. Data from the NBPA.

8. The middle-salary exception allows for a team to pay a player a mid-range salary even if it puts the team over the top.

9. The average salary in 1997–1998 is sometimes represented as $2.6 million. The $2.6 million figure includes only full-time roster players. The $2.4 million includes all players under contract.

10. The author served as a consultant to NBPA during 1998–1999.

11. See my elaboration of this point in "A Miami Fish Story," *The New York Times Magazine*, October 18, 1998.

12. Since it does not have a minor league system, the NBA's player development expenses principally consist of scouting and come to no more than 1 or 2 percent of the average team's expenses. On the economics of college basketball, see Zimbalist (1999).

13. This estimate was performed by Michael Ozanian, who had done similar estimates for all the major sports leagues for several years for *Financial World* before joining the staff at *Forbes*.

14. *Corporation Sourcebook of Statistics of Income*, 1990–1997; also in *Business Week*, various issues.

15. The actual system in football is to share the gate 60/40 after the home team has deducted 15 percent of the gross gate for theoretical stadium costs. Thus, the actual distribution of the gross is roughly 66/34.

16. Michael Ozanian, "Selective Accounting," *Forbes*, December 14, 1998, p. 127.

17. Year seven of the deal is at the owners' option. If they exercise the option, the 55 percent threshold rises to 57 percent in the seventh year.

18. The agreement actually calls for the introduction of a new revenue concept, Core Basketball Revenues or CBR. CBR will consist of gate receipts, all broadcasting revenue, luxury suite receipts, NBA properties revenue and certain other revenue to be determined. CBR will come into effect in the 1999–2000 season, and the BRI percentages will all be converted to a CBR basis.

19. For 1998–1999 the maximum player salary only affected two veteran players, Rik Smits in the senior category and Jayson Williams in the middle category (7–9 years of service). Ten players in the junior category, however, were affected with an average salary of around $12 million in the group over the lives of their contracts. These players were Shareef Abdur-Rahim, Ray Allen, Kobe Bryant, Zydrunas Ilgauskus, Allen Iverson, Stephon Marbury, Antonio McDyess, Arvydas Sabonis, Damon Stoudamire, and Antoine Walker.

20. Data are preliminary from National Basketball Players' Association.

21. Quoted in the *Sports Business Daily*, February 11, 1999.
22. I do not mean to suggest that the only cause of CBS' rating rise was its NFL contract, only that it helped. To be sure, it could not have hurt CBS when the Seinfeld show went off NBC after the 1997–1998 season.
23. A kind of reverse strategy was employed by the Seattle Mariners in 1997 and the San Diego Padres in 1998. In order to arouse public support for new stadiums, these teams fielded championship teams, only to dismantle them after their referenda for publicly funded new facilities had passed.
24. To be sure, it is likely that the NFL constraints on the salaries of franchise players are more severe than the $14 million cap (in 1998–1999) on veteran free agents in the NBA. Each NFL team can designate a franchise player. The services of this player can be automatically retained by the team if the player is offered compensation at the average of the top five paid players at his position in the NFL or 120 percent of the player' previous salary, whichever is greater.

References

Keteyian, Armen, Harvey Araton, and Martin Dardis. 1997. *Money Players: Days and Nights inside the New NBA*. New York: Pocket Books.

Quirk, James P., and Rodney D. Fort. 1999. *Hardball: The Abuse of Power in Pro Team Sports*. Princeton, New Jersey: Princeton University Press, p. 205.

Zimbalist, Andrew. 1999. *Unpaid Professionals: Commercialism and Conflict in Big-Time College Sports*. Princeton, New Jersey: Princeton University Press.

6

A Level Playing Field?
Sports and Discrimination

Lawrence M. Kahn
Cornell University

Economists and the public at large have become increasingly interested in the issue of discrimination in sports. The public perceives that
to some degree the sports business is an oasis of equal economic
opportunity for minorities, who in this setting are judged and compen-
sated solely on the basis of their performance. This impression is
underscored by the high level of minority representation in our major
team sports. As of the mid 1990s, Major League Baseball (MBL) was
about 30 percent black, the National Football League (NFL) was 65
percent black, and black players made up 80 percent of the National
Basketball Association's (NBA's) ranks (Staudohar 1996). Further,
some of the highest paid athletes are black: some multiyear NBA contracts for black players top $100 million; in baseball, a majority of the
players who made at least $8 million in 1998 were black, despite the
30 percent black representation in the MLB; and in the NFL, while
most of the highest paid players in 1997 were quarterbacks (a disproportionately white position, as I will discuss later), there were many
prominent, highly paid black players as well.

Despite this evidence of economic achievement, there is an omi-
nous undercurrent in the treatment of black professional athletes. Until
the 1940s, of course, black players were excluded from professional
team sports. And while African Americans are well-represented as
players in the 1990s, they are much less likely to be coaches, managers, or executives for sports teams. Anecdotal accounts of team sports
identify many instances in which African-American players perceived
quotas against them, even in basketball, which as noted, is overwhelm-
ingly black (Bradley 1976; Halberstam 1981). In 1987, a baseball

team executive claimed that black athletes did not have the qualities necessary to become managers or executives, and in 1988 a well-known broadcaster was fired for making racist comments (Staudohar 1996). Several players in the 1998 NBA lockout viewed the league's hostility as racially based (Samuels 1998). And golf and tennis, after years of being almost completely white sports at the professional level, still have few black players on tour. In many instances, tournaments in these sports have been played at clubs that do not accept African Americans as members.

Public attention focuses on issues of race and sports in part because of the celebrity of the players involved. Moreover, the history of racial integration in sports, beginning with the hiring of Jackie Robinson by the Brooklyn Dodgers in 1947 and soon continuing in football and basketball leagues has been an especially dramatic story. The process of racial integration in sports assumed national importance because it took place against the background of African Americans' struggle in the 1950s and 1960s for civil rights.

In this talk, I survey evidence economists have gathered on the extent of discrimination in sports. As I will show, discrimination can take on several forms, each of which has been the subject of economic research. Although the anecdotal evidence mentioned earlier is suggestive of the mistreatment of black players, we need to know what the anecdotes add up to. Are they isolated incidents, or are they symptomatic of general patterns and trends in professional sports? These questions can only be answered by studies that use statistical evidence. In this vein, I will talk about economic research on discrimination in sports with respect to salaries, hiring, retention, positional segregation, and customer prejudice.

ECONOMIC ISSUES IN ANALYZING DISCRIMINATION IN SPORTS

Before discussing evidence on discrimination in sports, it will be useful to make clear what I mean by "discrimination" and what economics has to say in general about the issue. Beginning with the seminal contribution of Gary Becker (1957), economists have usually defined labor market discrimination as the unequal treatment of equally qualified workers. Becker (1957) identified three forms of discrimination: employer, co-worker, and customer. As we will see, each of these forms has occurred in the sports business.

In the Becker model under competition, assuming profit-maximization by at least one firm and constant returns to scale, we expect entry and exit to eliminate employer and co-worker discrimination. Discriminating employers will be driven out of business by the nondiscriminator(s). As analyzed in Chapter 4 of Becker (1957), if there is co-worker discrimination, then in equilibrium we expect equally competitive segregated firms with equal pay for equal work. However, customer discrimination is different in that an employer who pays more money to workers whom customers prefer to deal with is likely to be rewarded by the market relative to one who does not make such distinctions. While workers not preferred by customers may be able to find work in the noncustomer sector, in a general equilibrium context, there is no guarantee that their incomes will not be hurt by the existence of customer discrimination (Kahn 1991a). And if these nonpreferred workers have a comparative advantage in the customer sector, then they may still choose to stay there even if they face the effects of customer discrimination.

These features of the economics of customer discrimination suggest that competitive forces are less likely by themselves to eliminate this form of discrimination than discrimination based on employer or co-worker prejudice. The sports industry is perhaps the most prominent example of a customer-based service sector. Further, because sports leagues are monopolies, they may not face the kind of free entry that might serve to discipline discriminating employers. Thus, we expect that the economic forces tending to eliminate discrimination in sports are perhaps weaker than in other industries.

A common difficulty labor economists have faced in testing for the existence of labor market discrimination is suggested by the definition I just explained. Namely, while it may be easy in many cases to tell who is paid more money, discerning if there is unequal pay for equally qualified workers can be a major problem. This difficulty has affected discrimination research on the labor force at large because databases such as those from the census can only tell us how many years of school a person completed, his/her age and marital status, and somewhat crude measures of where he/she works. For example, based on the census, the "productivity" of a 25-year-old minor league hockey player who played two years of college hockey is indistinguishable from that of a 25-year-old NBA star such as Magic Johnson, who turned pro after his sophomore year, and who in 1984 had already been the NBA finals' most valuable player (MVP) in 1980 and 1982. Is any pay gap between these two individuals evidence of unequal pay for equal work? In contrast to the census, in sports we have excellent controls for productivity, as indicated, for example, in *The Baseball Encyclopedia*. The sports industry provides us with an excellent opportunity to study discrimination because data on player race, compensation, and performance are so readily available.

EVIDENCE ON DISCRIMINATION IN SPORTS

In the early days of baseball integration, there was considerable evidence to support Becker's (1957) notions of employer, customer, and co-worker discrimination. First, employers discriminate if they treat the output of, for example, black workers, as less valuable than the identical output of white workers. If all employers have the same tastes for discrimination, then a common "discrimination coefficient" that describes this discount in dollar terms for the pay of black workers will result. A nondiscriminating employer can earn more money than a discriminator by hiring the most productive workers at the lowest cost possible, regardless of race, an opportunity that discriminators forgo. This prediction has been tested in the context of MLB's integration. Specifically, some teams, particularly those in the National League in the late 1940s and 1950s, were more active in bringing black players onto their rosters than were teams in the American League (Gwartney and Haworth 1974; Hanssen 1998). Teams that were more willing to use black players had significantly more success on the playing field than those that were not, an outcome predicted by Becker's (1957) model.

Second, there was some evidence of co-worker prejudice in the early days of baseball integration when the St. Louis Cardinals threatened to strike rather than play against a black player, Jackie Robinson.[1] Further, at least one Dodger player asked for a trade rather than play alongside Robinson, illustrating the tendency toward segregation, as predicted by Becker (1957). Third, there were many instances of customer prejudice, including death threats against Robinson in his early years with the Dodgers.

The labor market manifestation of these forms of discrimination can include salary discrimination (unequal pay for equal work), hiring discrimination, retention discrimination, and positional segregation. A considerable volume of research has attempted to determine the extent of these outcomes.[2] Salary discrimination is probably the most studied issue, with a research design that can be described by the following equation:

Eq. 1 $\ln S = B'Z + a\text{WHITE} + u,$

where for individual players in a given sport, S is compensation, B is a vector of regression coefficients, Z is a vector of performance indicators, team characteristics, and market characteristics, WHITE is a dummy variable equaling 1 for white players, and u is an error term. This setup is similar to much work in labor economics that attempts to assess the extent of discrimination by estimating a, the coefficient on WHITE.[3] What differs about sports is both the accuracy of the compensation data (that may in many cases come directly from the relevant players' union, which keeps copies of the actual player contracts) and the very detailed set of performance indicators available on athletes.

A major difficulty in conducting labor market research on discrimination using models like Eq. 1 is that WHITE may be correlated with unmeasured productivity, controlling for the measured variables Z; if so, then its estimated coefficient will be biased. In sports, we have much better controls than in labor market data in general. For example, a widely used data source such as the Michigan Panel Study of Income Dynamics (PSID) allows one to control for years of schooling, type of degree, length of labor market experience, firm seniority, union coverage, and three-digit industry and occupation classification. In contrast, the *Baseball Encyclopedia* and other baseball data sources allow one to control for batting average, stolen bases, home runs, career length, team success, and a variety of other performance indicators. In addition, "occupation" in baseball is one's position, a far more detailed indicator than exists in the census classification, which is used by the PSID. All players at the major or minor league level in all sports would get the same three-digit occupation ("athletes") and industry ("entertainment and recreation services") in the census classification. Because of far better controls for individual performance, occupation, and firm in sports, we presume that any correlation between WHITE and u, given Z, is much less severe in sports than in more general labor market data bases.

Analyses of equations like Eq. 1 have produced the most evidence of salary discrimination in professional basketball. In the mid 1980s, controlling for various performance and market-related statistics, there were statistically significant black salary shortfalls of 11–25 percent, depending on sample and specification.[4] The apparent discrimination was especially noteworthy because, as Table 1 shows, for the 1985–1986 season, black players on average earned $407,000, while whites earned $397,000. However, Table 1 also shows that black players out-did whites in major performance categories such as playing time, scoring, and rebounding. In fact, using a regression like Eq. 1, which controlled for performance and market-related variables, Kahn and Sherer (1988) found the *ceteris paribus* WHITE effect to be 21–25 percent, and this was highly statistically significant. This combination of results shows how important it can be to control for productivity, which

Table 1 Pay and Career Performance in the NBA

Year	Black players	White players
1985–1986		
Salary ($)	407,190	396,570
Minutes/game	25.45	20.86
Points/game	12.11	8.69
Rebounds/game	4.8	4.4
1994–1996		
Salary ($)	1,622,972	1,384,010
Minutes/game	23.9	18.7
Points/game	10.5	7.8
Rebounds/game	4.4	3.5

SOURCE: Kahn and Sherer (1988); Hamilton (1997).

in this case was higher for black players, in assessing the extent of discrimination. While variables may have been omitted that could have explained the *ceteris paribus* white salary advantage, reverse regression tests (which can under some restricted circumstances take account of such problems [Goldberger 1984]), showed even larger apparent discrimination coefficients (Kahn and Sherer 1988).

By the mid 1990s, there was evidence of unexplained black salary shortfalls only among the elite players in the NBA. Table 1 shows that, overall, blacks in 1994–1995 now outearned whites by about $240,000 and continued to outperform whites. Hamilton (1997) found for the 1994–1995 season that, all else equal, there were no overall significant racial salary differentials in the NBA. The point estimate in an ordinary least squares (OLS) regression like Eq. 1 was 0.010 for WHITE with a standard error of 0.093.[5] However, Table 2 shows that salary differentials were not uniform across the distribution. In particular, black players outearned whites through the 75th percentile, while among players near the top (the 90th percentile), whites were paid a slight $16,000 more than blacks. White stars did better relative to black stars than whites did among the journeymen. To examine the question of unequal pay for equal performance across the distribution of playing talent, Hamilton (1997) used quantile regressions like the following:

Eq. 2 $(Y_{90}|Z) = B_{90}'Z + a_{90} \times \text{WHITE}$,

where $Y_{90}|Z$ is the 90th percentile of conditional distribution of log salaries given Z and B_{90} and a_{90} are quantile regression coefficients. In

Table 2 Black and White NBA Salaries by Distribution Percentile, 1994–1995 ($)

Percentile	White players	Black players
10	150,000	270,000
25	250,000	752,000
50	1,036,500	1,417,500
75	2,135,000	2,333,500
90	3,260,000	3,243,800

SOURCE: Hamilton (1997).

particular, a_{90} tells us the WHITE log salary advantage for players at the 90th percentile of the conditional distribution of log salary.

Regressions such as Eq. 2 can be run for any distribution quantile, and the associated WHITE coefficients provide estimates of the unexplained salary premia for white players across the distribution. When Hamilton (1997) estimated models like Eq. 2, he found no significant racial salary differentials at the 10th, 25th, and 50th percentiles but positive and significant WHITE pay effects (at the 5.6 percent and 12 percent levels in two-tailed tests) at the 75th and 90th percentiles amounting to 0.18 to 0.19 log points.[6] These results suggest that while there was no significant unexplained black salary shortfall on average in the NBA in the 1994–1995 season, for star or near-star players (i.e., those at the 75th percentile and above in the conditional wage distribution), there may have been substantial discrimination in favor of whites. Again, the importance of controlling for performance is underscored because these white salary advantages are not apparent in Table 2, which, of course, does not control for performance.

In contrast to these findings of white pay advantage, *ceteris paribus*, in the NBA, similar OLS analyses of salaries in baseball and football have not found much evidence of racial salary discrimination against minorities. For example, in baseball, these analyses never find that being white has a positive effect. Among nonpitchers, in fact, significantly negative effects of being white were found in 1977 and 1987 (Christiano 1986 and 1988) and during the 1985–1991 period (Irani 1996). On the other hand, Kahn's (1993) analysis of 1987 data, using the same wage sample as Christiano (1988), found that these negative effects of being white disappeared when a longer list of productivity variables was added. In football in 1989, Kahn (1992) found *ceteris paribus* salary premia discrimination coefficients in favor of whites of only 1–4 percent, and these were usually not statistically significant. Kahn (1992) did find, however, that in the NFL, nonwhite players did better in areas with a larger relative nonwhite population than with a small relative nonwhite population; and whites did better in more white metropolitan areas. These findings suggest the influence of customers, but they did not add up to large overall racial salary differences in the NFL.

It is perhaps noteworthy that the one sport with the most evidence of racial salary discrimination, basketball, was the sport with the largest black representation as of the mid 1990s at 80 percent, in contrast to baseball's 30 percent and football's 65 percent.[7] These differences in racial representation suggest that customer preferences may have something to do with the racial pay gap we observed in basketball. And there is indeed evidence from the 1980s consistent with the existence of such preferences. For example, Kahn and Sherer (1988) found that, all else equal, during the 1980–1986 period each white player generated 5,700 to 13,000 additional fans per year. The dollar value of this extra attendance more than made up for the white salary premium.[8] And other researchers found a close match between the racial makeup of NBA teams in the 1980s and the areas where they were located, again suggesting the importance of customer preferences (Brown, Spiro, and Keenan 1991; Burdekin and Idson 1991; Hoang and Rascher 1999).

However, by the 1990s, customer preferences for white players were less evident. Dey (1997), for example, found that, all else equal, white players added a statistically insignificant and economically relatively unimportant 60 fans apiece per season during the 1987–1993 period. This evidence is consistent with the decline in the NBA's overall, unexplained white salary premium from the 1980s to the 1990s, although Hamilton's (1997) finding for whites near the top of the distribution still suggests fan preferences for big name white players. It is possible that white stars add fans even if the average white player does not.

Customer discrimination has also been found for baseball. For example, Hanssen (1998) found that white players added baseball fans, all else equal, for the 1954–1972 period, and Irani (1996) obtained a similar finding in baseball for 1972–1991. Moreover, Nardinelli and Simon (1990) found that, controlling for performance, in 1989, baseball cards for white players sold at a significantly higher price than those of black players, providing further evidence of fan prejudice. The lack of a white salary premium in baseball in the face of these customer preferences remains a puzzle. Perhaps the positional segregation and apparent retention discrimination in baseball (see the following paragraphs) are the ways in which such preferences affect the baseball labor market.

Other possible types of racial discrimination in sports involve hiring, retention, and assignment discrimination. These take the form of unequal probabilities of being drafted or retained, as well as positional segregation. First, regarding the draft, Kahn and Sherer (1988) found that there were small, insignificant racial differences actually favoring black players in draft order among NBA players on rosters in 1985, conditional on college performance. This suggested the absence of hiring discrimination in the NBA, but we had no information on those not drafted or not on rosters. In the NFL, Conlin and Emerson (1998) found indirect evidence that black players were drafted later than whites of equal playing ability during the 1986–1991 period. Again, without information on those not drafted or not making the roster, we have incomplete evidence on hiring discrimination. But Conlin and Emerson's (1998) results suggest barriers to black players in the NFL.

Second, regarding retention, Jiobu (1988) found that from 1971 to 1985 in Major League Baseball, black players had a significantly higher exit rate than whites, controlling for performance, position, and age at entry. Because baseball is likely to be virtually all major league players' best career opportunity, a reasonable interpretation of these exit hazard differences is that they reflect team decisions not to offer players a new contract. And Hoang and Rascher (1999) found a similar result for the NBA: Other things equal, during the 1980–1991 period, white players had about two additional years of career length (36 percent) than black players, again suggesting retention discrimination. Whether this disparity will hold up in the 1990s or whether, like the overall effects of race on attendance and NBA salaries, it will dwindle, is an interesting question for future researchers.

Third, positional segregation by race has been noted in baseball and football. Christiano (1988), for example, found that black baseball players in 1987 were overrepresented in the outfield and underrepresented at infield and catcher. Kahn (1992) found that in the NFL in 1989, nonwhite players were overrepresented at running back, wide receiver, and defensive back and underrepresented at quarterback, kicker, punter and offensive line (see Figure 1). Whether this segregation represents current discrimination, past discrimination by high school or college coaches, or self-selection is an open question, and there is lively but inconclusive debate about these issues (Kahn 1991b). Regardless of the cause of segregation, it appears to have some modest consequences toward a slight salary gap favoring white football players. Table 3 shows that the overall white salary advantage of 4 percent

Figure 1 Percent Nonwhite by Position, NFL 1989

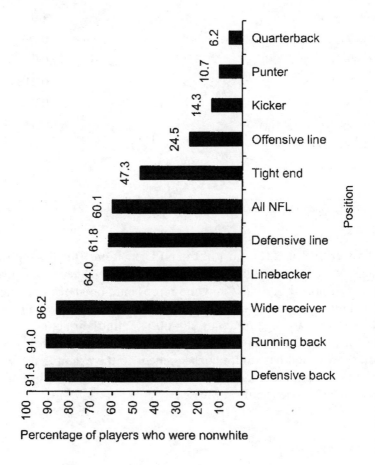

SOURCE: Data from Kahn (1992).

Table 3 White/Nonwhite Salary Ratio by Position, NFL 1989

Position	Players who were nonwhite (%)	White/nonwhite salary ratio
Punter	10.7	1.13
Offensive line	24.5	1.07
Defensive line	61.8	1.04
Tight end	47.3	0.99
Placekicker	14.3	0.96
Defensive back	91.6	0.94
Linebacker	64.0	0.91
Running back	91.0	0.69
Wide receiver	86.2	0.66
Quarterback	6.2	0.51
Total	60.1	1.04

SOURCE: Data from Kahn (1992).

is greater than it is for most of the NFL positions (the three positions where whites outearn blacks account for only 33 percent of the league). In fact, if nonwhites had the white representation at each position but kept their own position-specific salary levels, then they would outearn whites by an average of about $88,000. With their actual positional representation, nonwhites earned $13,000 less than whites. In baseball, segregation has future consequences to the extent that managers are drawn from the middle infield positions, which have been disproportionately white (Scully 1989). [9]

CONCLUSIONS

On the surface, it looks as though professional sports have come a long way since the 1940s when black players were banned from participating. As of the 1990s, African Americans are much more than pro-portionately represented at the major league level and earn on average millions of dollars in baseball and basketball. Further, pure salary discrimination, which may have been extensive in the 1980s in the NBA, appears to have declined by the 1990s and may currently be limited to white stars; and there is no evidence of salary discrimination in baseball and little in football. On the basis of these facts, one is tempted to conclude that discrimination in sports is a nonproblem.

Yet there is evidence that fans have or have had racial preferences in basketball, football, and baseball. Do these preferences have any consequences, as predicted by the economic theory of discrimination? The answer is that while overt salary discrimination is not a major outcome of these preferences (other than for the NBA in the 1980s or white NBA stars in the 1990s), there is some evidence that reflects hiring discrimination, positional segregation, and retention discrimination. With customer preferences continuing in many instances for white players and with evidence for these alternative forms of discrimination, professional sports and society at large have some distance to travel before they can say they have truly eliminated discrimination.

Notes

1. This discussion of race and baseball is based on Okrent and Wulf (1989) and Tygiel (1983).
2. For a survey of this evidence through the 1980s, see Kahn (1991b).
3. In some instances, researchers have used separate regressions for white and nonwhite players, reflecting or testing the possibility that performance is rewarded differently by race.
4. See for example, Kahn and Sherer (1988), Koch and Vander Hill (1988), Wallace (1988), and Brown, Spiro, and Keenan (1991).
5. Other analyses of basketball salaries in the 1990s also failed to find *ceteris paribus* racial salary differentials. See Dey (1997) and Bodvarsson and Brastow (1998).
6. The WHITE results for the lower percentiles were −0.184 (asymptotic standard error 0.291) for the 10th percentile, −0.209 (0.183) for the 25th percentile, and −0.005 (0.152) for the 50th percentile.
7. These figures were very similar in the 1980s as well. See Staudohar (1996).
8. Hoang and Rascher (1999) also examined NBA attendance during the 1980–1991 period and found that, other things equal, larger values of (percent white on the team/percent white in the city) were significantly positively associated with attendance. This finding is consistent with the idea of customer preferences for white players.

9. A lively literature has developed on the issue of discrimination against French Canadians in the National Hockey League. Some authors have found apparent discrimination against this group in Canadian cities outside Quebec province, a pattern consistent with the notion of customer discrimination (Jones and Walsh 1988; Longley 1995). Yet others have disputed this interpretation and the findings as well (Krashinsky and Krashinsky 1997). There is also a debate over whether French Canadians face entry barriers into the NHL, with some authors alleging that French Canadians need to have a higher performance level to be drafted as early as English Canadians (Walsh 1992; Lavoie, Grenier, and Coulombe 1992).

References

Becker, Gary S. 1957. *The Economics of Discrimination*. Chicago, Illinois: University of Chicago Press.

Bodvarsson, Örn, and Raymond T. Brastow. 1998. "Do Employers Pay for Consistent Performance?: Evidence from the NBA." *Economic Inquiry* 36(1): 145–160.

Bradley, Bill. 1976. *Life on the Run*. New York: Quadrangle/New York Times Book Co.

Brown, Eleanor, Richard Spiro, and Diane Keenan. 1991. "Wage and Non-wage Discrimination in Professional Basketball: Do Fans Affect It?" *American Journal of Economics and Sociology* 50(3): 333–345.

Burdekin, Richard C.K., and Todd L. Idson. 1991. "Customer Preferences, Attendance and the Racial Structure of Professional Basketball Teams." *Applied Economics* 23(1, Part B): 179–186.

Christiano, Kevin J. 1986. "Salary Discrimination in Major League Baseball: The Effect of Race." *Sociology of Sport Journal* 3(2): 144–153.

Christiano, Kevin J. 1988. "Salaries and Race in Professional Baseball: Discrimination 10 Years Later." *Sociology of Sport Journal* 5(2): 136–149.

Conlin, Mike, and Patrick M. Emerson. 1998. *Racial Discrimination and Organizational Form: A Study of the National Football League*. Working paper, Cornell University, Ithaca, New York.

Dey, Matthew S. 1997. "Racial Differences in National Basketball Association Players' Salaries: Another Look." *The American Economist* 41(2): 84–90.

Goldberger, Arthur S. 1984. "Reverse Regression and Salary Discrimination." *Journal of Human Resources* 19(3): 293–318.

Gwartney, James, and Charles Haworth. 1974. "Employer Costs and Discrimination: The Case of Baseball." *Journal of Political Economy* 82(4): 873–881.

Halberstam, David. 1981. *The Breaks of the Game.* New York: Alfred A. Knopf.

Hamilton, Barton Hughes. 1997. "Racial Discrimination and Professional Basketball Salaries in the 1990s." *Applied Economics* 29(3): 287–296.

Hanssen, Andrew. 1998. "The Cost of Discrimination: A Study of Major League Baseball." *Southern Economic Journal* 64(3): 603–627.

Hoang, Ha, and Dan Rascher. 1999. "The NBA, Exit Discrimination, and Career Earnings." *Industrial Relations* 38(1): 69–91.

Irani, Daraius. 1996. "Estimating Customer Discrimination in Baseball Using Panel Data." In *Baseball Economics: Current Research*, John Fizel, Elizabeth Gustafson, and Lawrence Hadley, eds. Westport, Connecticut: Praeger, pp. 47–61.

Jiobu, Robert M. 1988. "Racial Inequality in a Public Arena: The Case of Professional Baseball." *Social Forces* 67(2): 524–534.

Jones, J.C.H., and William D. Walsh. 1988. "Salary Determination in the National Hockey League: The Effects of Skills, Franchise Characteristics, and Discrimination." *Industrial & Labor Relations Review* 41(4): 592–604.

Kahn, Lawrence M. 1991a. "Customer Discrimination and Affirmative Action." *Economic Inquiry* 29(3): 555–571.

_____. 1991b. "Discrimination in Professional Sports: A Survey of the Literature." *Industrial & Labor Relations Review* 44(3): 395–418.

_____. 1992. "The Effects of Race on Professional Football Players' Compensation." *Industrial & Labor Relations Review* 45(2) 295–310.

_____. 1993. "Managerial Quality, Team Success and Individual Player Performance in Major League Baseball." *Industrial & Labor Relations Review* 46(3): 531–547.

Kahn, Lawrence M., and Peter D. Sherer. 1988. "Racial Differences in Professional Basketball Players' Compensation." *Journal of Labor Economics* 6(1): 40–61.

Koch, James V., and C. Warren Vander Hill. 1988. "Is There Discrimination in the 'Black Man's Game'?" *Social Science Quarterly* 69(1): 83–94.

Krashinsky, Michael, and Harry A. Krashinsky. 1997. "Do English Canadian Hockey Teams Discriminate against French Canadian Players?" *Canadian Public Policy–Analyse de Politiques* 23(2): 212–216.

Lavoie, Marc, Gilles Grenier, and Serge Coulombe. 1992. "Performance Differentials in the National Hockey League: Discrimination versus Style-of-

Play Thesis." *Canadian Public Policy–Analyse de Politiques* 18(4): 461–469.

Longley, Neil. 1995. "Salary Discrimination in the National Hockey League: The Effects of Team Location." *Canadian Public Policy–Analyse de Politiques* 21(4): 413–422.

Nardinelli, Clark, and Curtis Simon. 1990. "Customer Racial Discrimination in the Market for Memorabilia: The Case of Baseball." *Quarterly Journal of Economics* 105(3): 575–595.

Okrent, Daniel, and Steve Wulf. 1989. *Baseball Anecdotes.* New York: Oxford University Press.

The Baseball Encyclopedia. 1990. Eighth edition, New York: Macmillan.

Samuels, Allison. 1998. "Race, Respect and the NBA." *Newsweek*, December 21. Reprinted on *Newsweek* Web site www.newsweek.com.

Scully, Gerald W. 1989. *The Business of Major League Baseball.* Chicago: University of Chicago Press.

Staudohar, Paul D. 1996. *Playing for Dollars: Labor Relations and the Sports Business.* Ithaca, New York: Cornell University Press.

Tygiel, Jules. 1983. *Baseball's Great Experiment.* New York: Oxford University Press.

Wallace, Michael. 1988. "Labor Market Structure and Salary Determination Among Professional Basketball Players." *Work and Occupations* 15(3): 294–312.

Walsh, William D. 1992. "The Entry Problem of Francophones in the National Hockey League: A Systemic Interpretation." *Canadian Public Policy–Analyse de Politiques* 18(4): 443–460.

Author Index

An italic *f*, *n*, or *t* following a page number means the cited name is in a figure, note, or table, respectively, on that page.

Pechman, Joseph A., 54, 73

Quirk, James, 8, 18, 112n5, 113

Rascher, Dan, 123, 124, 127n8, 129
Rosentraub, Mark S., 26, 49, 52, 58, 73
Rottenberg, Simon, 17, 19

Samuels, Allison, 116, 130
Sanderson, Allen R., 26, 49
Scully, Gerald W., 126, 130
Sheehan, Richard G., 88, 91
Sherer, Peter D., 120, 120t, 121, 123,
      124, 127n4, 129
Shils, Edward, 46, 49
Siegfried, John J., 55, 61, 73
Simon, Curtis, 123, 130
Spiro, Richard, 123, 127n4, 128
Staudohar, Paul D., 116, 127n7, 130
Sweeney, George H., 55, 61, 73

Tygiel, Jules, 127n1, 130

Vander Hill, C. Warren, 127n4, 129

Wallace, Michael, 127n4, 130
Walsh, William D., 128n9, 129, 130
Wulf, Steve, 127n1, 130

Zimbalist, Andrew, 26, 49, 52, 53, 73,
      112n12, 113
Zimmerman, Dennis, 52, 58, 71n2, 73

Subject Index

An italic *f*, *n*, or *t* following a page number means the subject information is in a figure, note, or table, respectively, on that page.

Government
  federal government tax subsidies for
    stadiums, 52, 55
  See also Congress; Local/state
    government
Government policy. *See* Public policy
Graduation rates for college athletes, 89*t*
Grantham, Charlie, 105
Gross economic impact, of stadiums on
    neighborhoods, 26–27
Gross expenditures for sports events,
    45*n*1
Gross versus net financial inflows, 33
  for Seattle, King County, and
    Washington state, 26

Hardball (Fort and Quirk), 8
Hiring discrimination in pro sports,
    123–124, 127
Hockey
  income levels of fans, 67*t*, 68, 69, 70
  salary caps, 111
  team owners' reaction to NBA
    settlement, 106
  World Hockey Association (WHA),
    16
  See also National Hockey League
Holmes, Justice Oliver Wendell, 11
Hotel and motel tax subsidies for
    stadiums, 54–55
Hotels, located near stadiums, 42
Huizenga, Wayne, 108
Hunter, Billy, 105–106

Ice hockey. *See* Hockey
Income
  of buyers of tickets to sports events,
    61–63, 62*t*, 67*t*
  CES' top-coded level of, 62
  of fans of particular sports, 63–68
  of nonbuyers of tickets to sporting
    events, 61–62, 62*t*, 67*t*, 68
  team owners', 56
  See also Players' salaries; Revenues

Indiana Pacers, 68
Internet, effect on pro sports, 18
Invariance principle, 17
Jobs, claims that stadiums create new, 28
Joint venture sale of TV rights, 9, 11
Jordan, Michael, 94–95, 104, 106

King County, Washington, impact of pro
    sports on, 26
Kingdome
  economic impact on Pioneer Square,
    29–35
  economic impact on Pioneer Square
    business revenues, 39*t*, 40, 42–43
  questionnaire about, 47–48
  survey results, 36–43
  team owners' dissatisfaction with,
    27–28

Larry Bird exception, 94–95
  owners' call for elimination of,
    96–97
Leagues
  average owners' assets and player's
    salaries in 1998, 56
  breaking up of existing, 16, 94, 111
  cooperation among team owners, 12,
    93
  creating economically competitive,
    12–18, 94
  management of the number of teams
    in, 11
  mergers among, 15
  minor, 17
  monopoly profit earned by, 9–10
  monopoly rights, 10–11
  special legal treatment of, 8, 11 ·
  start-up costs for new, 15
  tendency towards a single monopoly,
    14
  See also Pro teams; Revenue

About the Institute

The W.E. Upjohn Institute for Employment Research is a nonprofit research organization devoted to finding and promoting solutions to employment-related problems at the national, state, and local levels. It is an activity of the W.E. Upjohn Unemployment Trustee Corporation, which was established in 1932 to administer a fund set aside by the late Dr. W.E. Upjohn, founder of The Upjohn Company, to seek ways to counteract the loss of employment income during economic downturns.

The Institute is funded largely by income from the W.E. Upjohn Unemployment Trust, supplemented by outside grants, contracts, and sales of publications. Activities of the Institute comprise the following elements: 1) a research program conducted by a resident staff of professional social scientists; 2) a competitive grant program, which expands and complements the internal research program by providing financial support to researchers outside the Institute; 3) a publications program, which provides the major vehicle for disseminating the research of staff and grantees, as well as other selected works in the field; and 4) an Employment Management Services division, which manages most of the publicly funded employment and training programs in the local area.

The broad objectives of the Institute's research, grant, and publication programs are to 1) promote scholarship and experimentation on issues of public and private employment and unemployment policy, and 2) make knowledge and scholarship relevant and useful to policymakers in their pursuit of solutions to employment and unemployment problems.

Current areas of concentration for these programs include causes, consequences, and measures to alleviate unemployment; social insurance and income maintenance programs; compensation; workforce quality; work arrangements; family labor issues; labor-management relations; and regional economic development and local labor markets.